Personal Finance Workbook for Beginners

Personal
Finance Workbook
for Beginners

Practical Exercises for Smarter Money Management and Financial Empowerment

Dylin Redling and Allison Tom

ROCKRIDGE PRESS

First Rockridge Press trade paperback edition 2022

Rockridge Press and the Rockridge Press logo are trademarks or registered trademarks of Callisto Media Inc. and/or its affiliates in the United States and other countries and may not be used without written permission.

For general information on our other products and services, please contact our Customer Care Department within the United States at (866) 744-2665, or outside the United States at (510) 253-0500.

Paperback ISBN: 978-1-63878-697-9 | eBook ISBN: 978-1-68539-345-8

Manufactured in the United States of America

Interior and Cover Designer: Jenny Paredes
Art Producer: Melissa Malinowsky
Editor: Alexis Sattler
Production Editor: Melissa Edeburn
Production Manager: David Zapanta

All images used under license from Shutterstock; author photo courtesy of © Monica May Design

10 9 8 7 6 5 4 3 2 1 0

For our wonderful family
and friends, our favorite teachers,
our fur babies (Lele and Lukey),
and our 25-year-old selves,
who knew nothing about finances
but were willing to work hard
and enjoy the ride.

Contents

Introduction

Hello! We're Dylin Redling and Allison Tom, and we hope you're excited to learn all about the wonderful world of personal finance. It's a subject that has not traditionally been taught in most schools, yet it's one of the most important elements of your life. When we were in school, we didn't learn about practical things like getting a job, buying a home, or planning for retirement. Instead, we had to figure out our personal finances the hard way, through trial and error.

After we began our careers in the tech industry in San Francisco in the late 1990s, we were able to pay off our student loans and start investing in our employers' 401(k) plans. We changed jobs many times, often negotiating promotions and salary increases along the way.

In 2009, severe pneumonia put one of us in the intensive care unit for 10 days. The silver lining was that this near-death experience forced us to reevaluate our lives and our goals. We became more interested in our personal finances and began investing strategically in stocks and bonds and buying and selling real estate. Eventually, we paid off our mortgage. We made it a goal to retire early, and we were able to do so through thoughtful financial decisions over the next decade.

That brings us to this book and how it will help you. We realize that people reading this will be coming from different backgrounds, with various levels of knowledge. Our goal is to make personal finances easy to understand by explaining complex topics in clear and simple ways and keeping the content grounded in the real world. To reinforce each topic, we've created activities, quizzes, and exercises that complement the subject matter in each chapter.

No matter your age or socioeconomic background, it is never too late to learn the basic concepts of personal finance and work to improve your financial life. This book is designed to make it easy to learn what are often seen as complex concepts.

How to Use This Book

This book is structured so that each section builds on the previous one, progressing from simpler concepts to more complicated ones. However, the book is also assembled so that you can flip directly to a chapter or specific topic to find the exact information you seek, such as information on buying a home or planning for retirement.

Imagine that your financial journey is like a cross-country road trip. Part one of this book resembles the preparation phase, where you map out your route and tune up your vehicle. In this section, you'll get a taste of the basics of personal finance, assess where you are, and make a plan to build your financial foundation.

Part two resembles the driving portion of the trip, during which you experience all the twists, turns, and obstacles. Each chapter will help you navigate one big piece of your financial life, from managing debt to investing for your future.

On a road trip, you may encounter destination checkpoints and scenic vistas along the way. In this book, these vistas come in the form of educational activities using tools like quizzes, checklists, and budget templates. These activities will help put your plan into action.

Throughout the journey, be patient with yourself. Some of this book's concepts are complex. However, if you open yourself up to learning new things, you may make some surprising discoveries. Make sure to appreciate the journey!

PART I

Essential Steps to Get Started with Personal Finance

One of the most difficult aspects of being a beginner and learning something totally new is simply getting started. The sooner you begin, the faster you can pay off debts and start growing your money.

Keeping in mind the metaphor of the cross-country road trip, consider this the preparation stage. First, you map out your route. Then you figure out where to stop along the way. And before you drive off, you can tune up the car, top off the gas, and check the tire pressure for the long journey ahead.

Part one of this book will help you do similar preparation for your financial journey. You'll examine your relationship to money and how your priorities and behaviors influence your finances. Then you'll assess your priorities to help you set realistic and attainable goals. Finally, you'll learn which steps to take to set up your all-important financial foundation.

CHAPTER 1

Focus on the Person in Personal Finance

There is a reason it's called "personal" finance. Your finances are unique to you: influenced not only by your background and socioeconomic status, but also by your habits, priorities, and behaviors. In this chapter, you will discover how these traits shape your relationship to money and impact your financial life.

Everyone has memories, good or bad, of their early interactions with money. If someone's parents or caregivers constantly argued about the household finances, then discussing money could make them anxious. For others, they may have fond memories of earning their first dollars from a paper route or lemonade stand. Reflecting on your personal relationship to finance, and how it has influenced your financial habits and behaviors, is the first step on your journey.

In this chapter, you will discover why finances are difficult for everyone, no matter their background or level of financial literacy. You'll learn why it's important to engage intentionally with your finances, as opposed to going through your financial journey without a plan.

If you were preparing for a cross-country road trip, you would likely gauge how comfortable you feel and how prepared you are, so you can plan accordingly. This chapter is the equivalent of checking in with yourself on your finances.

Kevin's Shopping Habit

K evin has been slowly climbing the corporate ladder at work. He is 35 years old with two school-age kids at home, and much of Kevin's career ambition is to provide a good life for his kids.

He loves his job, but it can certainly get stressful at times. He has 12 associates reporting to him, rigid deadlines, and an unforgiving boss. To alleviate the stress, Kevin has gotten into the habit of going to the local shopping mall during his lunch hour.

Exploring the different department stores, pricing clothes, and trying things on gives Kevin a mental break from the demands of his job. What started as leisurely browsing has turned into a regular purchasing habit. Kevin justifies his purchases with the belief that they will help his career. He needs to look polished and professional to get his next promotion.

As his wardrobe starts to overflow, Kevin begins to reconsider his shopping habit. Then he discovers the clearance section, and his mindset switches to one of not wanting to miss out on a sale.

Eventually the costs of Kevin's shopping habit start to catch up with him. Reviewing his credit card statements, he realizes he can't afford to keep buying clothes he doesn't need, even at sales prices. He decides to bypass the store on his next lunch break and walk outside instead. Ultimately, he finds the walks help alleviate his stress in much the same way as perusing the sales rack, but without the price tag.

When Finance Is Personal

Your personal finances encompass a wide variety of activities and decisions you make about your money. It includes any income you generate, the money you use to pay for groceries, and the investments you make so you can retire someday.

Many people don't consciously think about their money decisions. As you travel through your financial journey, try to be intentional with your money by thinking about how your habits may affect you in the long run. Let's look at some examples.

Without an intentional plan for your money, you may go to work each day hoping your boss sees that you're trying hard and will offer you a raise. You go to the grocery store without a list and buy whatever looks enticing. Since you're not tracking your spending, you can't be sure you're putting away money for the future. You can see how this approach to financial success isn't the best.

With an intentional plan for your money, you would create a 6-to-12-month strategy to get a promotion or raise. You set up a budget for your household expenses and highlight areas that could be comfortably trimmed or with which you have difficulties. You make a plan to start building an emergency fund and eventually a retirement account.

As you continue learning about financial concepts, you will become more mindful about your earning, spending, and saving. This awareness will lead to more confidence about your money decisions and better overall financial health.

Personal Finance Is Difficult for Everyone

Personal finance is one of the most difficult aspects of life. It is like planning a road trip: You are trying to create a path from where you are to where you want to go. Because you're not given a road map at birth, finding your way can be difficult without some guidance.

Very few schools offer personal finance education, and not everyone has the same advantages or the same access to information. Many people simply don't have family or friends who can explain how to invest in stocks or how credit scores work. Everyone has a unique upbringing and situation, and that's why personal finances are *personal*.

Financial challenges come in many forms, including controlling spending and maintaining financial self-discipline. According to a 2007 study by Yankelovich, a market research firm, the average consumer is exposed to as many as 5,000 ads per day! Just think about all the ads you come across on social media, search engines, television, radio, and billboards.

Less-controlled spending can have a domino effect on your finances. You spend more, which increases your debt, and that in turn reduces the amount you could be saving. Fortunately, you can overcome these obstacles by acquiring the knowledge to make better financial decisions.

What Your Relationship to Your Finances Reveals about You

Examining your relationship with money can be illuminating and give you a better understanding of how your values and interests relate to your finances. For example, does money excite you or overwhelm you? Are you patient when facing financial difficulties, or do you get easily frustrated? Do you find money talk interesting or boring? There are no wrong answers here, as long as you're being honest with yourself.

Your spending and overall relationship to money reflect your priorities, thoughts, and habits, many of which are unconscious. For example, if you have always ordered take-out food, then you may not even consider that you could save money by preparing your own meals. Ordering food becomes a habit that eventually affects your finances.

Going back to Kevin: His clothes-buying behavior became a habit that impacted his life in a variety of ways. What started as an innocent practice slowly turned into a more destructive habit, even though the sales prices made it feel like he was being a smart consumer.

What does Kevin's relationship to his finances reveal about him? It certainly shows that his job is stressful, and that he is driven to succeed in his career to help his family. It also indicates a tendency to spend habitually without much thought. Fortunately, if you are mindful about your financial behaviors, you can make positive changes. Kevin was able to find ways to get his mental health break without breaking his financial bank.

To Change Your Finances, You First Have to Examine Your Priorities and Behavior

Learning about personal finance is wonderful, but it can only take you so far without good habits to help you apply this knowledge consistently. To really improve your financial situation, it's important to understand what motivates your money decisions. Think of it as "Financial Psychology 101."

The decisions you make can be influenced by your life experiences, your values, and your personality. Some factors that affect how you relate to money include:

PRIORITIES AND VALUES. These often take the form of long-term goals or powerful motivations. When making a decision, they outweigh other concerns to tip the scales. Family, health, a hobby, work-life balance, friendship—there's no wrong answer when it comes to what you choose to prioritize.

THOUGHTS AND BELIEFS. This is everything you were taught or told about finances throughout your life. It could be that all debt is bad, that you should stay loyal to one employer throughout your career, or that investing is overly complicated. These beliefs can either empower you or limit you.

HABITS AND BEHAVIOR. If priorities and values are motivations, then habits and behaviors are the routines designed consciously or subconsciously to get you there. For example, if you value health, then you may go to the gym regularly and eat healthy foods. If friendship is a priority, then you may spend your weekends going out to dinner with your friends.

Self-analysis in these areas will help you identify your financial motivations and provide you with the necessary adjustments to improve your finances over time.

There's No Shame in Being a Beginner

Even the most amazing outcomes can come from very humble beginnings. For instance, several major companies started in a garage, including Apple, Hewlett-Packard, Google, Amazon, Disney, and Mattel. There is absolutely no shame in being a beginner at anything, especially when it comes to personal finance.

In fact, you should embrace your "beginner's mind." Zen Buddhism even has a term for it called *shoshin*. It refers to having an attitude of openness, eagerness, and lack of preconceptions when studying a subject. If you start with this mindset, you open yourself up to getting the most from the material you're learning.

Think about when you were a child in preschool or kindergarten, and everything was fresh and new. Or, if there are children in your life, think about how they approach learning right now. Young kids absorb new concepts such as drawing, counting, and socializing like a sponge. You can find that beginner's mindset again, no matter what your current circumstance might be.

As you go through the rest of this book, try to bring a sense of curiosity and self-compassion into the learning process. Your relationship to money and finances is a lifelong journey, so be patient and enjoy the ride.

This Book Will Help Guide You

Before you go further, you should take a moment to congratulate yourself! The fact that you are holding this book right now means you are already prioritizing your financial well-being. By taking this first step, you'll be honing skills such as initiative, research, and long-term thinking, all of which are needed to take control of your finances.

This book not only will provide you with the knowledge you need about your personal finances, but also will guide you on how to use what you've learned so that you can face down any future financial questions with confidence. It's designed to be personalized to help you on your financial journey, from building your foundation to planning for retirement. Throughout the book, you'll have the opportunity to apply the information you've learned to your personal situation.

Personal finance concepts can be somewhat complex, but if you are willing, you can learn them. You can become comfortable wielding the fundamental tools to improve your financial life, even if you're starting as a complete beginner.

You could have stayed at home, but instead you made the important decision to embark on this big adventure. Now you just need to map out your journey, put together your packing list, and get your vehicle ready before taking off!

Financial Beliefs Checklist

Your beliefs about money matters can have a tremendous effect on your finances. They can be either empowering or limiting.

Below is a checklist with examples of both types of beliefs. Go through each one and check the ones that apply to you. Remember, there's no right or wrong answer. This exercise is simply to gauge where you are right now.

Limiting beliefs:

☐ All debt is bad.

☐ Salary is the only thing to focus on when applying for a job.

☐ It's always better to own my home.

☐ I don't need to worry about retirement planning until I'm older.

☐ All investments are risky.

Empowering beliefs:

☐ Some debt can help me get ahead.

☐ There are specific actions I can take to get a promotion.

☐ Renting my home can sometimes be better than buying.

☐ I can plan for retirement when I'm young.

☐ Investing doesn't have to be overly complicated.

Note that many of the limiting beliefs use words like "all" and "always." Empowering beliefs use terms like "some" and "sometimes." This distinction is important. Many financial decisions are gray areas in which there isn't a hard-and-fast rule about what to do. Although those gray areas might make your decisions harder, they also increase your opportunities for success.

Now that you have an idea of different empowering and limiting money beliefs, you can create your own list. Think about what you've been taught or have heard about finances throughout your life. It could be something your parents or caregivers believed, something you learned in school, or perhaps something you saw on television or read about.

Write down your money beliefs, and then put a (+) for an empowering belief or a (-) for a limiting belief. By identifying the negative thoughts, you will be able to adjust your thinking as you gain knowledge.

Consumers are constantly bombarded with messages about buying various goods and services. Advertisers are paid lots of money to convince you to spend, spend, spend. As a result, it's easy to make purchases unconsciously and buy things you may not really need.

Think about a time you regretted spending money on a purchase. What was your mindset before you paid? When did your feelings about the expense shift and why?

How Your Spending Reflects Your Values

If your purchases match your values, you can feel more comfortable that you're making the best choices with your money. This exercise will show you what you're doing well and what you could do better to align your spending habits with your values.

Below are several expense categories that take into account most of the spending of the typical household. Under each category, identify a value and list expenses that you currently make that reflect this value. Perhaps you prize protecting the environment. In the category of transportation, you could list expenses for owning an electric vehicle or taking public transit.

As you go through your spending habits, consider how you could be spending differently to meet your values. If your expenses don't currently reflect your values, how could you change your spending to better support them?

Housing Value: ....

Housing Expenses: ....

Transportation Value: ....

Transportation Expenses: ....

Food Value: ....

Food Expenses: ....

Entertainment Value: ....

Entertainment Expenses: ....

Other Value: ....

Other Expenses: ....

Are Your Habits Costing You Money?

Everyone has money-spending habits. Some habits can sabotage your savings. It's important to learn about and be aware of these hindering habits.

To get a sense of how your spending habits may be affecting your finances, answer the following by circling either "True" or "False."

1. I dine out fewer than five times per week. (True or False)

2. I create a meal plan for the week. (True or False)

3. I make a shopping list when I go grocery shopping. (True or False)

4. I avoid impulse buys when I shop. (True or False)

5. I can remember all my monthly subscriptions without looking (e.g., streaming services, gym membership, etc.). (True or False)

6. I avoid clicking on ads when surfing the Internet. (True or False)

7. I pay my credit card bills in full every month. (True or False)

Tally up the number of times you answered "True." Here is a gauge to see where you'll want to place your future focus:

0 to 2: You may be in a place to prioritize letting go of habits that no longer serve you and to create space for new ones.

3 to 5: You already have some supportive habits in place; keep up the momentum as you explore even more.

6 to 7: Put your energy toward reinforcing those useful habits you've already developed.

Conscious vs. Unconscious Spending

It can be helpful to inventory your current expenses and see how aware you are about your spending. Although it's not necessary to have a rigid plan, you'll usually be in better financial shape if you budget your expenses.

In the table below, list your top expenses, based on total cost. Then identify each as a "want" or a "need" and whether you spend "consciously" or "unconsciously" on each. Spending consciously means you are aware of your spending and understand why you're making this expense. When you spend unconsciously, you make your payment each month without thinking about the expense and whether it's beneficial to your financial health (for example, a gym membership you rarely use).

EXPENSE	WANT OR NEED	CONSCIOUS OR UNCONSCIOUS
Ex: Rent or mortgage	Need	Conscious

For any unconscious expenses, think about how you might be able to be more mindful about your spending. You could set aside a budget for entertainment or do more price comparisons before your next trip.

Key Takeaways

This chapter delved into the *personal* aspect of personal finance and how your personality, behaviors, and motivations affect your finances. Improving your financial situation involves understanding why and how you make your money decisions. It's also important to align your spending with your core values.

Main takeaways from this chapter:

√ Your finances are unique to you. They are influenced not only by your background and socioeconomic status, but also by your habits, priorities, and behaviors.

√ Your thoughts and beliefs about money can either be limiting or empowering. Identifying these beliefs is the first step to reducing the number of limiting beliefs.

√ A common pitfall is spending on autopilot; however, by being more conscious of your spending, you can put yourself in the driver's seat.

√ Embrace your *shoshin* or "beginner's mind" when it comes to personal finance. Approach the learning process with curiosity and self-compassion.

It's never too late to learn the financial fundamentals, whether you are just getting into the workforce or are closer to retirement age. Keep your beginner's mind open as you go into the next chapter, where you can start mapping out your financial goals.

CHAPTER 2

Assess Where You Are and Decide Where You Want to Go

I n this chapter, you will take stock of your current financial situation and formulate a vision for your future. To assess where you currently are, you will run a diagnostic test of your financial health. This self-check will include a wide variety of financial metrics, such as your debt-to-income ratio, credit score, and net worth. You'll also take inventory of your short-term emergency fund and assess your long-term retirement plans. From there, you'll evaluate where you want to go by looking at your priorities and setting up attainable short- and long-term goals.

If that sounds like a lot, don't worry, because you'll be provided the opportunity and resources you need to become familiar with each category before you make an assessment.

Imagine what you would do to set your priorities and goals for your road trip. Do you want to take the scenic route and see the Grand Canyon or Mount Rushmore on the way, or would you prefer to arrive at your destination as soon as possible? Similarly, you are in control of your financial journey. You get to make the decisions at each step of this journey to get to your desired destination.

Jonathan's Financial Wake-Up Call

Jonathan is 26 years old and works as a server at a trendy downtown restaurant. He's happy to have flexibility in his schedule from week to week, and he likes his coworkers.

Recently, Jonathan started dating Leslie, who is the manager of a high-end clothing store near the restaurant. He was very excited for their first date and took her to his favorite sushi restaurant, followed by the latest blockbuster sci-fi movie. Although Leslie had a great time and enjoyed Jonathan's wit and charm, she was a bit taken aback by how he treated his money.

Jonathan's restaurant is popular, so he's usually too busy during his shifts to worry about organizing his tip money. He simply stuffs the various bills into each of his pants pockets without thinking much about it.

Years of working in retail have conditioned Leslie to be very methodical with cash. She decides to teach Jonathan what he would later call the "wallet lesson." Leslie shows him how to be more mindful with his money by neatly organizing his cash in denominational order and folding the bills in his wallet. It's a very simple lesson, but one that makes a big impact on how Jonathan thinks about his finances.

For the first time in his life, Jonathan realizes how important it is to respect his money and the hard work that goes into earning it. He creates a budget, sets up a savings plan, and begins to think about his long-term financial situation.

The Measures of Financial Health

Assessing your financial health is a lot like gauging your physical health. When you go to the doctor, they ask you questions about your family history and daily habits. They check your height, weight, blood pressure, cholesterol, and glucose levels.

When evaluating your financial health, you will be looking at a variety of factors, such as your debt, income, credit, assets, liabilities, and savings. It might seem overwhelming at first, but to improve your financial situation, it's important to know where you are now.

Financial health looks different for people at different stages of their life. A recent college graduate may have a lot of debt, no credit, and low income. Someone closer to retirement age may have more savings and more established credit. Facing facts is brave, and it's important not to judge yourself. No matter what you learn about your financial health, this book will provide you with guidance for how to adjust accordingly.

Debt-to-Income Ratio

Your debt-to-income ratio is the percentage of your total monthly income, called *gross* income, being allocated to pay your monthly debt payments.

To calculate your debt-to-income ratio, add up your monthly debt payments—including mortgage, credit cards, and any loans—and divide that number by your gross monthly income, before taxes and deductions.

Mortgage lenders use this ratio to determine your ability to manage loan payments. Most prefer the ratio to be less than 35 percent, but may consider offering a loan for somebody with a ratio up to 43 percent.

Preparedness for Financial Emergencies

You never know when you might have a large, unexpected expense. One day your refrigerator could stop working, you could find yourself facing a lawsuit, or you could experience an injury that leaves you with steep medical bills.

In the event of a financial emergency, you will want to have cash on hand that is easy to access, in a savings account for example. The usual rule of thumb is to create an "emergency fund" with enough money to cover all your household expenses for three to six months. If your monthly expenses are $3,000, then you would want to have between $9,000 and $18,000 available.

Credit Score

Your credit score is used by creditors to determine how risky it would be to lend you money and how likely you are to pay it back. A good score can help you get a home or car loan, better interest rates, or additional credit.

If you have a variety of different credit card and loan accounts, a history of on-time payments, and low balances on your credit cards, companies feel like they have a clear picture of your financial behavior.

Credit scores range from 300 to 850. Generally, a score under 580 is considered poor, 580 to 669 is fair, 670 to 739 is good, and 740 and above is excellent. Keep in mind that no matter what your score is now, you *can* improve it over time by, among other things, consistently making on-time payments.

There are several ways to get your credit report. You can check with the Consumer Financial Protection Bureau at ConsumerFinance.gov for more information.

Net Worth

Your net worth is a measure of the total value of your financial assets after subtracting your debts. Net worth is one of the most common gauges of personal financial wealth. When someone is referred to as a millionaire, that means their net worth is greater than $1 million. When you're starting out, your net worth may even be negative.

To calculate your net worth, add up the value of all your assets such as your home, automobile, cash, investment accounts, and high-value personal items. Then subtract all your liabilities—the debts you owe, including your mortgage, car loan, and other loans.

Retirement Savings and Investments

Retirement plans are savings accounts that offer tax advantages to help and encourage you to invest for your later years. Your employer may offer a retirement plan, such as a 401(k) plan, or you can set up your own Individual Retirement Account (IRA) by contacting a financial institution.

Both types of plans make it easy to set aside a small portion of your income during your working years. Your contributions are invested in a bank, an investment company, or an online brokerage. The tax advantages allow you to either contribute with before-tax money via a traditional account or withdraw tax-free via a Roth account.

COMMON MYTHS AND MISCONCEPTIONS ABOUT FINANCIAL HEALTH

Now that you understand the key metrics around financial health, let's discuss some of the myths and misconceptions.

A low debt-to-income ratio means you are in control of your expenses. Just because you don't have a lot of debt doesn't mean you can afford your expenses. You may not have loans, but the amount you spend on rent and other expenses or hobbies may keep you from saving.

A credit card counts as an emergency fund. When used responsibly, credit cards can be an easy and effective way to make purchases. However, relying on credit rather than an emergency savings fund for unexpected expenses can put you in a hole of high-interest debt.

Once you have a bad credit score, you cannot rebuild it. Although it's true that late or missed payments can stay on your credit report for up to seven years, it's never too late to boost your score. As you begin making your payments on time, you can improve your overall history.

Net worth is the only metric that matters. Yes, your net worth is important as a measure of your available wealth. However, it's only a snapshot of your current situation. If your other metrics are not what they could be, then your net worth can quickly take a turn for the worse.

You can wait to contribute to your retirement accounts. The earlier you start saving for retirement, the more your money will grow. Contributing a small amount from your current paycheck can set you up for a more comfortable retirement.

Understanding these misconceptions can help you make smarter financial decisions throughout your life.

Take Stock of Your Priorities

Now that you've assessed your financial health, you have some information on which areas you may need or want to prioritize. To avoid feeling overwhelmed, you can work on your financial health in stages.

Imagine you're putting together a giant jigsaw puzzle. First, you must find a work area that fits the puzzle with plenty of light. Then you could turn all the pieces up and start grouping and sorting them. You might work on the corners first, and then the edges, and finally the center, before connecting everything. In this same way, you can improve your financial health step by step.

You won't be able to address all your financial health metrics at once. Typically, you would focus on your debt first. Continuing to maintain a lot of debt, especially high-interest-rate loans, can keep you from making progress toward your personal financial goals. As you're paying off your debt, make sure not to miss or be late with any payments. Doing so will improve your credit score.

Next, concentrate on your earnings and income. By increasing the money coming in, you'll be able to better handle your debts and start saving. Once you have your emergency savings, you can set aside part of your income for retirement account contributions.

You can see it's a logical progression from first managing your debt and decreasing your expenses to then growing your income and ultimately your savings. Later in the book, you will learn more specific strategies for tackling each of these financial health metrics.

Set Attainable and Realistic Goals for the Short and Long Term

Now that you have an understanding of the key financial health metrics, it's time to work on setting some goals. A great tool to help you is the acronym SMART.

S = SPECIFIC. It will be difficult to hit your goal if it's too vague. For example, if your goal is *"to get rich,"* how do you know when you've achieved it? A clearer goal might be *"to have a net worth of $1 million by age 40."*

M = MEASURABLE. It's important to be able to measure your goal so you have a clear understanding of where you want to go. In the previous example, you can measure your net worth goal by subtracting your liabilities from your assets.

A = ATTAINABLE. It's vital to set goals that are attainable and realistic. If your goals are unattainable, then you'll get frustrated when you don't achieve them. Each time you reach a short-term goal, it pushes you ahead to aspire toward your longer-term goals.

R = RELEVANT. You have the right short-term goals if those goals help you reach your long-term goals. For example, if you'd like to have a net worth of $1 million by age 40, you might want to set an interim goal of being out of debt or increasing your monthly savings to a specific amount by a certain age.

T = TRACKABLE. Once you know how to measure your goal, you should also be able to monitor its progress. In the net worth example, you could create a spreadsheet with all your assets and liabilities and update it on a regular basis.

Think about what some financial goals might look like for you. For now, don't worry about whether they adhere to the SMART criteria; just write down whatever goals come to mind. Your goal could be to improve one of your financial health metrics, or you could set a larger goal such as acquiring a college degree or buying your first home.

Making a SMART Financial Goal

In this exercise, you will take one of your financial goals and apply the SMART goal-setting technique.

Let's say your goal is to "Improve my debt-to-income ratio." You would then expand and elaborate on that goal to meet the SMART criteria. Your SMART goal may become: "To improve my current debt-to-income ratio from 40 percent to 20 percent in 10 years."

Using the space below, brainstorm and redesign a new goal by explaining how it can meet each of the SMART criteria.

Original Goal: _____

S = Specific: _____

M = Measurable: _____

A = Attainable: _____

R = Relevant: _____

T = Trackable: _____

New Goal: _____

When you're ready, you can do this exercise for all the goals from the previous exercise. Hopefully this will give you more confidence that these are the right goals for you. From there, you can put together strategies and plans to achieve each one.

Rate Your Financial Health Metrics

Now that you're familiar with some of the most important financial health metrics and how to calculate them, evaluate how you're currently doing with each one.

This exercise will help illustrate which areas to apply your focus and which areas are in better shape. After each statement, choose the answer that best describes your situation.

My debt-to-income ratio is:

a.   43 percent or greater

b.   30 percent to 42 percent

c.   Less than 30 percent

d.   Don't know

My emergency fund has:

a. $0

b.   Up to two months of expenses

c.   More than two months of expenses

d.   Don't know

My credit score is:

a.   Less than 650

b.   650 to 700

c.   Over 700

d.   Don't know

My net worth is:

a. $0 to $100,000

b. $100,000 to $500,000

c. Over $500,000

d. Negative

My retirement savings account balance is:

a. $0

b. Up to $100,000

c. Greater than $100,000

d. Don't have an account

Scoring:

How did you do? Were you circling more *a*'s than you expected? Did you surprise yourself with how many *c*'s you had? Don't worry if you're not satisfied with some of your answers. That's why you're reading this book!

Myths about Financial Health

In this chapter, you learned about several myths and misconceptions around financial health metrics. For example, a credit card does not count as an emergency fund, and your net worth is not the only metric that matters.

Look at some additional statements and answer each of the following statements by circling either "True" or "False."

1. Investing requires a lot of money. (True or False)

2. Credit cards should always be avoided. (True or False)

3. It's always better to own my home. (True or False)

4. A low debt-to-income ratio is a sure sign that I am in control of my expenses. (True or False)

5. More income equals more wealth. (True or False)

6. Large debts should always be paid off first. (True or False)

All these statements are FALSE. What's important is to understand why they're all false. Remember that there are a lot of gray areas with finances. Rarely is a statement true for all people and all circumstances.

Short- and Long-Term Financial Goals

To achieve your desired financial future, it's helpful to have both short- and long-term goals. In this exercise, imagine where you would like to see yourself in three years, 10 years, and 20 years.

Start by entering your financial metrics for the present day in the categories of debt-to-income ratio, retirement savings, and net worth. Then look toward incremental improvement over each time period. Consider how much you can realistically improve at each juncture and feel empowered to aim high in the 10- and 20-year projections. As you make effective financial decisions in the coming years, the payoff will start to compound, and the results could be exponential!

TIME FRAME	DEBT-TO-INCOME RATIO	RETIREMENT SAVINGS	NET WORTH
Example	38%	$350,000	$640,000
Present Day			
3 Years			
10 Years			
20 Years			

Just putting down projected numbers won't magically make them happen. However, if you have some clear and realistic targets to shoot for, then you can create the necessary strategies to get there.

You've had a chance to think a lot about your short-term and long-term financial goals and aspirations. Now allow yourself to have some fun with your goals. Imagine what your life might look like if you were to achieve everything on your list.

Would you be totally debt free, living on a boat in the Caribbean? Or would you own your own business doing something you love? Feel free to be creative and dream big!

Key Takeaways

This chapter was about measuring and evaluating your financial health metrics in preparation for achieving your financial goals. It's like conducting a complete diagnostic test on a vehicle before a big road trip to see what needs to be fixed or tuned up.

The main takeaways from this chapter:

√ Key metrics include your debt-to-income ratio, emergency fund, credit score, net worth, and retirement savings.

√ To improve your financial health, it's helpful to first prioritize which areas need the most attention, and then work on making incremental changes.

√ Beware of financial health myths such as "a credit card counts as an emergency fund" and "net worth is the only metric that matters."

√ A great tool for setting goals is the SMART technique (Specific. Measurable. Attainable. Relevant. Trackable.)

Your understanding of financial health metrics and goal setting will help in the next chapter, where you'll discover how to build your financial foundation.

CHAPTER 3

Make a Plan to Stabilize Your Foundation

This chapter will cover some of the practical steps you can take in the short term to stabilize your personal finances and build a foundation for future growth. These steps include important financial practices such as creating a budget, building an emergency fund, and paying down high-interest-rate debt.

By going through a preparedness checklist with your finances, you will be ensuring you have the basics covered for your financial journey. Your planning in the short term will help you set up a strong foundation for the long term. For example, rather than focusing on becoming a millionaire, first focus on getting your high-interest debt under control. Although it's important to take these steps seriously, it's also key to approach them with self-care in mind. Being patient with yourself will help you stay motivated and on track with your financial goals.

Consider this the part of your road trip when you map out your first pit stops. You will have researched where to stop for a meal, where to fill up the tank, and where to stay each night. This planning will ensure you have the basics covered for your long journey.

Monika and Mohamad's Lake Tahoe Retirement Dream

Monika and Mohamad have big dreams about what they want to do in retirement. They are currently in their early 30s, recently married, and enjoying their respective careers. Mohamad is a human resources professional, and Monika is a lieutenant in the San Francisco Fire Department.

Their ultimate goal is to retire by age 60 with an apartment in the city and a cabin at Lake Tahoe. They imagine skiing in the winter, boating in the summer, and enjoying city life in spring and fall.

They realize that now is the time to start getting serious about their finances if they want to make their retirement dream a reality. They decide to focus on three things: creating a budget, paying down Mohamad's high-interest-rate student loan debt, and setting up their retirement account contributions.

To start tracking their expenses, they create a shared spreadsheet that they can both contribute to and monitor. Even though they have access to employer-sponsored retirement plans, they haven't started contributing yet. They had put it off thinking that they would have more time to do it later, but "later" never seemed to arrive. They make a promise to finally set up their contributions this quarter.

It's just a start, but these initial steps feel good. Monika is dreaming about the fresh snow she'll be skiing down, and Mohamad can't wait to relax on the lake.

Short-Term Steps to Build a Financial Foundation

Having big dreams is wonderful. In fact, it would be difficult to have a successful future if you couldn't first imagine it. However, achieving big dreams requires setting and achieving smaller goals along the way.

Monika and Mohamad's case study is an illustration of why it's so important to lay a sturdy financial foundation before chasing your bigger dreams. If they continued their current trajectory with no game plan, not only would they not reach their big goal, but they may even find themselves going deeper into debt.

Each of their established goals fit into the SMART goal-setting model. They are specific, measurable, attainable, relevant to their bigger retirement goal, and trackable.

Next, look at some of the short-term steps you can take to build *your* financial foundation.

Build a Budget You Can Stick To

The word "budget" turns a lot of people off, because it feels like you'll have to deprive yourself of all the good things in life. However, just like exercise and nutrition is necessary for good physical health, spending wisely is required for good financial health.

If it helps, don't think of it as "cutting your spending," but rather "spending smarter." Break your spending into buckets such as housing, food, transportation, loans, insurance, and entertainment. First put your current spending in each bucket. Then think about how you could reduce, or shift, your expenses in each category without negatively affecting your happiness.

Start an Emergency Fund

An emergency fund is typically three to six months' worth of expenses that are easily accessible, such as in a savings account. You want this buffer so that you don't have to take out a loan or go into debt if a large, unexpected expense comes your way.

Even if it takes you a year or longer, you can slowly start putting money away into this fund until you have enough. Once it's there, you hopefully won't have to worry about it again, unless you have an actual emergency. However, if you must use that money, make sure to replenish the fund.

Prioritize Paying Down High-Interest-Rate Debt

High-interest-rate debt, such as credit cards, can slow your momentum in two ways. First, you're paying back more than you borrowed to the lender as a premium for offering you credit. Second, it's an opportunity cost. The money you are paying back to a lender is money you don't have the chance to grow and invest for your own benefit.

For these reasons, it makes sense to pay down your high-interest-rate debt as quickly as you can. If you have credit card debt, make a plan to eliminate that first, since those rates are typically the highest.

Insure Your Health and Your Property

Making sure you have sufficient insurance goes hand in hand with your emergency fund to provide you with financial protection against the unexpected. The two main categories of insurance are insurance for yourself and insurance for your property.

Insurance for yourself includes healthcare coverage, long-term disability, and life insurance that provides your beneficiaries with a sum of money when you die. For your property, insurance provides coverage for your residence, automobile, and other belongings.

You can purchase any of these plans on your own. If applicable, you can also check with your employer to see if it offers any insurance coverage as part of your employee benefits.

Start Saving for Retirement, Even If Your Contributions Seem Small

Due to the power of compound interest, the earlier you start planning for your retirement the better. The way compound interest works is that you are paid interest by your financial institution, which adds to the amount you've already invested. So, the next time you earn interest, it will be calculated using the same percentage rate but applied to your new, larger cumulative total. You earn interest *on top* of interest, which is essentially free money!

To illustrate how compound interest works, if you were to invest $10,000 at a 10 percent annual interest rate, that one-time investment would be worth $452,592.56 after 40 years.

COMMON MYTHS AND MISCONCEPTIONS ABOUT SHORT-TERM FINANCIAL PRIORITIES

Setting up your finances in the short term is very important but can be tricky. Let's take a look at some of the myths and misconceptions about these short-term financial priorities.

Building a budget means tracking every penny you spend. Although it doesn't hurt to track everything, you'll make the most progress by focusing on your largest expenditures. The 80/20 rule applies here: 80 percent of your expenses are likely coming from 20 percent of your spending categories, such as housing, transportation, and food.

There's time to build an emergency fund when you are making more money down the road. The fact is that your emergency fund is more important in the early stages, because you don't have additional resources if something happens.

Paying down debt can hurt your credit score, so it's better to carry a balance on your credit card. The amount of interest you pay to a credit card lender does *not* affect your credit score, but it certainly hurts your savings.

You don't need to insure your health and property. Perhaps you think that you're healthy and careful, so you don't really need insurance. The truth is that two of the biggest causes of bankruptcies in the United States are large, unexpected health and property expenses.

You can't access your retirement savings until you reach retirement age. The IRS allows penalty-free withdrawals from traditional retirement accounts after age 59.5, but there are ways to withdraw retirement contributions in your earlier years. For example, you can withdraw contributions from a Roth IRA without penalty at any age.

The First Step Is the Most Important

How you plan your initial steps will depend on your situation. When it comes to finances, assume you can't afford to wait. So, rather than succumb to analysis paralysis, remind yourself that what matters most is moving forward even if the steps are small.

Although the right first step depends on your personal circumstances and everyone is different, here are some initial steps you can take in each of the main categories highlighted in this chapter:

BUILDING A BUDGET. Start by tracking your expenses either in a spreadsheet or with old-fashioned pen and paper. Go through your recent bank statements and make a list of all your spending for the month.

EMERGENCY FUND. Calculate what three months of expenses would be and determine how much money you'd need to set aside each month for a year to get to that point.

PAYING DOWN HIGH-INTEREST-RATE DEBT. Before you pay your debts, you need to face them. Start by recording all your debts by amount, lender, and interest rate.

INSURING YOUR HEALTH AND PROPERTY. Research and compare the costs and coverage of insurance plans, especially for healthcare and property insurance.

SAVING FOR RETIREMENT. Look into your options for setting up a retirement account. If applicable, check to see if your employer offers a 401(k) or equivalent plan. If not, then look into opening an IRA account.

Any one of these can be the right first step for you, if it gets you moving forward on your path rather than standing still.

Remember That You're Doing This for You

Once you start taking these initial steps to build your financial foundation, you'll begin to gain some momentum and feel better about your finances. You can continue that momentum and stay on the path by remembering that you are doing something for yourself.

It can be difficult to set a budget and pay off debt. Human beings typically prefer spending money to saving it. Spending provides immediate satisfaction, but having patience, perserverance, and self-discipline will help you make better financial decisions.

It's like when you were in school. If you want to graduate, you must have a plan, go to class, do your homework, and stick to it consistently. However, when the weekend rolls around, you might want to take a break to recharge. The same can be said of your financial health plan. It's perfectly reasonable to treat yourself occasionally.

Perhaps you've been trying to save money by preparing all your meals at home. That's an admirable goal, but it's also a lot of work. If you allow yourself a meal out every now and then, you won't be totally depriving yourself, and you may appreciate those experiences even more.

It's important to be patient with yourself while you are working on your financial foundation. If you have a setback, don't beat yourself up over it. Allow yourself some grace and resume your plan. Your future self will thank you for all the work you're doing today!

It can be difficult figuring out the initial steps to take to build your financial foundation. If you feel frozen with inaction, one exercise to help you "break the ice" is to identify the obstacles holding you back.

Think about the five initiatives discussed: building a budget, creating an emergency fund, paying down debt, getting necessary insurance, and starting to contribute to retirement. Ask yourself if there are any you feel reluctant to try. Why? Are there roadblocks you anticipate?

Your Financial Foundation

You learned quite a bit in this chapter about setting up your financial foundation. The more you know about these personal finance essentials—budgeting, saving, and insuring—the better positioned you'll be to begin your financial journey.

Answer each of the following statements by circling either "True" or "False."

1. I should aim for an emergency fund of 3 to 6 months of expenses. (True or False)

2. It's better to wait to pay off my high-interest-rate debt. (True or False)

3. I don't need healthcare coverage if I'm young and healthy. (True or False)

4. Because of compound interest, the sooner I start investing the better. (True or False)

5. I don't necessarily have to track every penny when building out my budget. (True or False)

6. Paying down debt can hurt my credit score. (True or False)

7. It's possible to withdraw contributions from a Roth IRA without penalty at any age. (True or False)

Understanding these concepts can give you the knowledge and support you need to build out your all-important financial foundation.

Answers:
1. *True*
2. *False (you should pay off your high-interest-rate debt as soon as possible)*
3. *False (illnesses or accidents can be costly and affect anyone at any age)*
4. *True*
5. *True*
6. *False (paying down debt does not affect your credit score)*
7. *True*

Your Current Budget

Throughout this chapter, you have learned about and taken the initial steps to build out your budget. You will now put pen to paper and write out your complete current monthly budget. Remember, it's okay if your spending is not ideal right now. This part of the process is for assessing where you currently are so you can make improvements in the future.

To complete this exercise, it can be helpful to gather up your most recent bank and credit card statements. Review your monthly expenses to put together an accurate picture of your spending, and then put a total at the bottom. Note that these are just some of the most common expenses, and you may not have an expense in each row.

CATEGORY	MONTHLY EXPENSE
HOME	
Mortgage or Rent	$
Insurance	$
Property Taxes	$
Utilities	$
Homeowner's Association (HOA) Fees	$
Other Home Expenses	$
TRANSPORTATION	
Gas	$
Insurance	$
Parking	$
Tolls	$
Public Transit (subway, bus, train)	$
Other Transportation Expenses	$

CATEGORY	MONTHLY EXPENSE
FOOD	
Groceries	$
Dining Out	$
Other Food Expenses	$
ENTERTAINMENT/RECREATION	
Movies	$
Cable TV/Streaming Services	$
Hobbies (equipment, memberships, classes)	$
Events (concerts, sports, etc.)	$
Other Entertainment Expenses	$
PERSONAL/FAMILY	
Healthcare	$
Child Care	$
Education	$
Clothing	$
Other Personal Expenses	$
MISCELLANEOUS	
Loan/Debt Payments	$
Donations/Philanthropy	$
Other Misc. Expenses	$
TOTAL EXPENSES	**$**

Changes to Your Monthly Budget

Now that you've put together your current monthly budget, this exercise will help you make a few adjustments to it.

In the column "Changes," select a few categories that you may be able to reduce or redistribute to other areas. For example, perhaps you're currently spending $200 per month on dining out, but you think you could cut that to $100 by buying $50 more in groceries.

CATEGORY	CURRENT BUDGET	CHANGES	NEW BUDGET
HOME			
Mortgage or Rent	$	$	$
Insurance	$	$	$
Property Taxes	$	$	$
Maintenance	$	$	$
Other Home Expenses	$	$	$
TRANSPORTATION			
Auto Loan	$	$	$
Gas	$	$	$
Insurance	$	$	$
Parking	$	$	$
Tolls	$	$	$
Other Transportation Expenses	$	$	$

CATEGORY	CURRENT BUDGET	CHANGES	NEW BUDGET
FOOD			
Groceries	$	$	$
Dining Out	$	$	$
Other Food Expenses	$	$	$
ENTERTAINMENT/RECREATION			
Movies	$	$	$
Cable TV/Streaming Services	$	$	$
Gym/Fitness Classes	$	$	$
Events (concerts, sports, etc.)	$	$	$
Other Entertainment Expenses	$	$	$
PERSONAL/FAMILY			
Healthcare	$	$	$
Child Care	$	$	$
Education	$	$	$
Clothing	$	$	$
Other Personal Expenses	$	$	$
MISCELLANEOUS			
Loan/Debt Payments	$	$	$
Donations/Philanthropy	$	$	$
Other Misc. Expenses	$	$	$
TOTAL EXPENSES	$	$	$

Financial Foundation Action Checklist

Your budget is only one aspect of your financial foundation. It's important to also address your savings, debt, and insurance.

Below are three first steps you can take for each of the other financial priorities. Check them off once you complete them.

Emergency fund:

☐ Tally up current total cash savings.

☐ Review monthly take-home pay.

☐ Calculate a dollar amount you could reasonably save each month.

Paying down high-interest-rate debt:

☐ Record all your outstanding loans and debts.

☐ Determine the interest rate for each debt.

☐ Pay off more than your minimum for the loan with the highest rate for one month.

Insuring your health and property:

☐ Review which insurance policies you currently hold.

☐ Inquire if your employer offers any insurance with your benefits.

☐ Research the marketplace and identify options if your employer doesn't offer insurance.

Saving for retirement:

☐ Mark down any retirement accounts you already have set up.

☐ Check if your employer offers a 401(k) plan (or equivalent).

☐ Enroll and make at least one contribution payment in any amount.

Each time you make a check mark, you're getting one step closer to building your financial foundation!

Think again about the five initiatives discussed: building a budget, creating an emergency fund, paying down debt, getting necessary insurance, and starting to contribute to retirement. Everyone starts with a different level of financial preparedness. Depending on where you are currently, you may have more or less work to do on these initiatives.

Try to imagine how it would feel to have this foundation fully built to your own specifications. What emotions or feelings do you have in this future scenario? Does it make you more confident about your finances?

Key Takeaways

It's so important to set up this solid foundation at the beginning of your financial journey, no matter when that may be. Imagine trying to build a house without a proper foundation; it wouldn't last very long in a big storm or natural disaster!

Here are the main takeaways from this chapter:

√ Setting short-term financial goals is the basis for building your financial foundation.

√ Beware myths such as "you have to track every single expense" and "you cannot access any of your retirement account funds until age 60."

√ The sooner you start building out your financial foundation, the better.

√ It's important to be patient with yourself while you are working on your financial foundation.

Congratulations on making it through part one of this book! You now have the essential steps to get started with personal finance. In part two, you will build on your financial foundation and learn how to create a financially healthy life.

PART II

Building a Financially Healthy Life

In this section, the rubber meets the road. You'll take off on your journey and start exploring how you can deal with debt, maximize your employment and earnings, understand your options for renting versus owning a home, plan for retirement, and invest for your future.

As you learn about each of these topics, imagine that they are stops along your personal journey. Perhaps your plan is to visit all the major national parks, or maybe you want to find the best burger joints in each state. Just like a big road trip will have twists, turns, ups, and downs, your financial journey will have various obstacles to overcome. By the end, you will have all the tools you need to successfully navigate this adventure.

CHAPTER 4

Dealing with Debt

I t is challenging to get much traction on other facets of personal finance if you are saddled with debt. Picture yourself trying to get started on your big road trip, and you notice you have four flat tires, there's no gas in the tank, and you haven't had an oil change in 10,000 miles. You're not going anywhere until you inflate your tires, fill up the gas tank, and get an oil change.

The same goes for dealing with high-interest debt. For example, it wouldn't make sense to start investing your savings somewhere, even if you could get a return of 10 percent, when you could use that savings to more quickly pay off a debt that has an interest rate of 15 percent. You need to pay off that high-interest debt first, and then you can start socking away money into savings and investments.

In this chapter, you'll learn about the different types of debt, how to manage them, and how to use debt to your advantage. You'll find out that some types of debt can actually help you build wealth in the long run! The key is understanding how to leverage your debt properly.

Erik's Mountain of Debt

Erik is 22 years old and about to graduate from college. He is looking forward to getting out into the professional world, but he is concerned about the $50,000 debt he's racked up during his college career. He wonders, *"How did my debt get so out of hand?"* Thinking back over the past four years, Erik starts to put it all together.

It started his freshman year when Erik felt he never had enough money for meals, textbooks, or activities with friends. He heard about a credit card that had no annual fee and a 0 percent interest rate for the first six months. Unfortunately, the interest rate increased to 18 percent after the introductory period. By his junior year, Erik had maxed out his credit card with a balance of $15,000.

During his senior year, Erik got a part-time job off campus and needed a car to commute. Erik took on a $10,000 auto loan at 9 percent interest. On top of his credit card and auto loan debt, Erik amassed another $25,000 in student loan debt, but at a lower 4 percent interest rate.

Erik finally decided to ask his mother, a financial consultant, for some advice. The first thing his mother did was tally up the balances and respective interest rates. Then she introduced Erik to the "avalanche method," where he would pay the highest-interest-rate debt first while making minimum payments on the other loans. It will take some time and dedication, but Erik now has a plan for conquering his debt.

The Double-Edged Sword of Debt

Think about doing your big road trip on a motorcycle. It requires different training, experience, equipment, planning, and preparation than driving a car. However, if you are an experienced rider, have a motorcycle that's in great shape, and wear the necessary protective gear, then you could have an amazing experience on your bike. Managing debt is much the same; it can be great if you manage it well, but it can be risky if you're not careful.

The good side of debt is that you can use it to help you build your long-term wealth. One example is a mortgage loan to help you buy your home or purchase an investment rental property. Another example is a student loan that helps you get the education you need for a particular job or to reach a specific career goal after college.

The downside of debt is paying interest rates that, if you can't pay them down quickly enough, may spiral out of control. Some of the riskiest debt is credit card debt. Using credit cards is fine if you pay off your balance each month. It's a convenient way to pay for things, and you can even get rewarded with cash back or points for travel. However, if you don't pay off your balance each month, then you're paying some of the highest interest rates in the industry. The average credit card interest rate as of February 2022 was 16.17 percent. That is why in the chapter example, Erik's mother advised him to pay off his $15,000 of credit card debt before his student loans and auto loan.

Common Types of Debt

Debt comes in a variety of shapes and sizes, from credit cards and student loans to car loans and mortgages. They differ based on factors such as how and when you use them, their interest rates, and their level of riskiness. Chances are that you have had or will have one or more of these types of debt in your lifetime.

You don't always have a choice about taking on debt. Sometimes it's necessary or unavoidable. For instance, if you want to go to college or own a home, you'll most likely have to borrow money to do so. If you find that you do have to take on some debt, it's important to select the right type of debt and have a strategy to pay it off.

In the following sections, you'll learn more about the different types of debt, the average interest rate for each, and when and how to use each one.

Credit Cards

Credit card debt is the riskiest type of debt because the interest rates are so high. Depending on the type of card, APRs (annual percentage rates) have historically fluctuated anywhere from 14.99 percent to 23.99 percent. The rates can be even higher if you have a low credit score.

With rates that high, why would anyone use credit cards? If you pay off your balance in full each month, then you don't pay any interest, so it's essentially an interest-free loan for 30 days. Other advantages include convenience, reward points like cash back and travel points, insurance coverage, travel benefits, and the ability to improve your credit score.

Student Loans

Student loans can be a less risky type of debt. First, the interest rates are much lower. From 2013 to 2022, the federal undergraduate interest rate ranged from 2.75 percent to 5.05 percent, and the rates are fixed for the life of the loan.

Second, you are essentially using the loan to invest in your future earning potential. This is unlike credit card debt, which is more often accrued to pay for day-to-day items that have short-term use. Of course, there is no guarantee that your education will result in a high-paying or fulfilling job, but the potential upside may outweigh the possible downside.

Car Loans

Depending on your credit score and the type of vehicle you're purchasing, the interest rate on an automobile loan can vary widely. From 2019 to 2021, the average rate for a new car ranged from 4.05 percent to 5.38 percent. For used cars, it ranged from 7.98 percent to 9.03 percent, since sellers need to recover the costs from trade-ins, such as cleaning, refurbishing, and repairs.

Although new car loan rates may seem reasonable, you should be mindful about the amount of debt and monthly payments you're taking on. In 2021, the average new car loan was $37,280 with a monthly payment of $609.

Medical Debt

There may be times when you need or want a medical procedure that is not covered by your health insurance. In these circumstances, you might consider getting a "medical loan," which is a personal loan that is used for medical or dental expenses.

Common uses for medical loans are cosmetic surgeries, fertility treatments, elective surgeries, and prescriptions. Depending on your credit score, interest rates for medical loans typically range from about 5 percent to 9 percent.

When making decisions about whether to take out a medical loan, it's advisable to consult with medical professionals and prioritize your health as best you can.

Mortgages

Mortgage loans, which are used to purchase a home, have several advantages over other types of debt. First, you can typically obtain a lower interest rate for a mortgage loan than for other types of loans. The average interest rate for a 30-year fixed mortgage between 2019 and 2021 ranged from 3.0 percent to 3.9 percent.

Second, you're able to deduct some of the mortgage interest from your taxable income on your federal income tax return. And finally, you're buying a valuable asset rather than spending money on rent. Just be aware that homes can lose value as well!

COMMON MYTHS AND MISCONCEPTIONS ABOUT DEBT

It can be tricky to navigate the world of debt and credit. You have to know which debts are riskiest, which loans will support your long-term goals, and how your actions affect your credit score and ability to obtain future credit.

Some common myths and misconceptions about debt include:

All debt is bad. Some types of debt are useful and can help you get ahead, such as student loans for your college education and mortgages to help you purchase a home.

Checking your credit report will hurt your score. When you check your score, it's called a "soft inquiry" and does *not* affect your credit score in any way. A "hard inquiry" is when a creditor pulls up your credit information, and that *does* affect your credit score temporarily.

Using credit cards is bad. If you pay your credit card bill in full each month, you won't pay the high interest rate on your balance. This way you can enjoy the convenience and benefits of using credit cards without the negative side effects.

You make too much to qualify for federal student loans. There is no income requirement for federal student loans. Many families don't apply because they falsely believe they won't qualify.

If a lender approves you for a car or home loan, you can afford it. Just because you can get a loan doesn't mean you should. It's important to make sure that you can comfortably afford the monthly payment, as well as other costs such as insurance, maintenance, and gas or taxes.

Managing Debt

It's easy for debt to spiral out of control; however, there are strategies you can use to tackle it. Two that work well are the "avalanche method" and the "snowball method." With both strategies, you first list out all your debts, their interest rates, total debt amount, and minimum payments. Next, you focus on aggressively paying down one of your debts while making minimum payments on the others to avoid late charges.

With the "avalanche method," you focus on paying down the debt with the highest interest rate first. This method can save you more money, as you will be paying less interest over time. Using the "snowball method," you pay off the smallest balances first to get them out of the way. This method works well psychologically, since you get to see the number of outstanding debts disappear quicker.

If you find that your debt is simply unmanageable, you can look to debt consolidation, debt settlements, credit counseling, or bankruptcy. Debt consolidation allows you to combine multiple debts into a single loan. With debt settlement, you negotiate with your creditors to accept less than the total amount owed.

Nonprofit credit counselors are free and can help you manage your debt and create a budget. And if nothing else works, you may be able to file for bankruptcy. Doing so will clear almost all your debts, but can remain on your credit report for up to 10 years and make it more difficult to get a loan or a credit card.

Test Your Knowledge about Debt

This chapter has given you a crash course in debt. Now's your chance to take stock of what you know and what you might want to keep reviewing.

For each question, circle the statement that applies:

1. **Which of the following statements about using a credit card is false?**
   a. Makes purchasing easier
   b. Some offer reward points
   c. Can help me improve my credit score
   d. Interest rates are low

2. **Which of the following statements about student loans is false?**
   a. They can be used for buying a car
   b. Undergraduate interest rates are lower
   c. Graduate interest rates are higher
   d. Interest rates for federal loans are fixed

3. **Which of the following statements about car loans is false?**
   a. Used car interest rates are higher
   b. New car interest rates are higher
   c. In 2021, the average monthly car payment was over $600
   d. They can be used for electric vehicles and SUVs

4. **Which of the following statements about mortgage loans is false?**
   a. I can deduct mortgage interest on my tax return
   b. Interest rates are relatively low
   c. I don't have to pay it back if I lose my job
   d. My home is an asset that can appreciate over time

Answers: 1-d, 2-a, 3-b, 4-c. How did you do?

To navigate to an end goal, you have to truly understand where you stand at the current moment. Getting your debt under control is no exception.

In the space below, think about your current level of debt. Does it bring up any particular emotions? Do you currently feel confident about your ability to improve your debt situation? Why or why not?

Using the Avalanche Method to Pay Down Your Debts

The "avalanche method" is one of the most effective strategies for paying down your debts. In this exercise, you will input your debts in order from highest to lowest interest rate. Then you will consider how much more you could pay each month toward the debt with the highest interest rate, based on your current income.

Here is an example:

TYPE OF DEBT	CURRENT DEBT AMOUNT	INTEREST RATE (HIGH TO LOW)	MINIMUM PAYMENT DUE	PROPOSED MONTHLY PAYMENT
Credit Card	$10,000	18%	$100	**$200**
Car Loan	$5,000	5%	$200	$200
Student Loan	$25,000	4%	$400	$400
Total	**$40,000**		**$700**	**$800**

In this example you'd pay off your credit card debt first because it has the highest interest rate.

Now, it's your turn. See what it looks like when you put your own debt information into the table. Then think about how much more you could comfortably pay each month toward the highest interest rate debt.

TYPE OF DEBT	CURRENT DEBT AMOUNT	INTEREST RATE (HIGH TO LOW)	MINIMUM PAYMENT DUE	PROPOSED MONTHLY PAYMENT
	$	%	$	$
	$	%	$	$
	$	%	$	$
	$	%	$	$
Total	$		$	$

Using the Snowball Method to Pay Down Your Debts

In this exercise, you will input your debts in order from lowest to highest debt amount. Then you will consider how much more you could pay each month for the smallest total debts.

Here is an example using the same debts from the previous exercise, but now ordered by debt amount:

TYPE OF DEBT	CURRENT DEBT AMOUNT (LOW TO HIGH)	INTEREST RATE	MINIMUM PAYMENT DUE	PROPOSED MONTHLY PAYMENT
Car Loan	$5,000	5%	$200	$300
Credit Card	$10,000	18%	$100	$100
Student Loan	$25,000	4%	$400	$400
Total	**$40,000**		**$700**	**$800**

In this example you'd pay off your car loan first because it has the lowest balance. In the "Proposed Payment" column, you increase your car loan payment from $200 to $300 while keeping the other minimum payments.

Now, try using the snowball method with your debts. Then think about how much more you could comfortably pay each month toward debt with the smallest balance.

TYPE OF DEBT	CURRENT DEBT AMOUNT (LOW TO HIGH)	INTEREST RATE	MINIMUM PAYMENT DUE	PROPOSED MONTHLY PAYMENT
	$	%	$	$
	$	%	$	$
	$	%	$	$
	$	%	$	$
Total	$		$	$

After looking at both methods, the avalanche and the snowball, give some thought as to which one would work better for you.

Cutting Through the Myths about Debt

You've absorbed a lot of information about debt in this chapter. It's important to identify what is myth and what is reality if you are to reach your financial goals.

See how much you remember by circling "True" or "False" for each of these statements:

1. The average credit card interest rate as of February 2022 was 10 percent. (True or False)

2. If I pay off my credit card balance in full each month, then I don't pay any interest. (True or False)

3. Federal undergraduate student loan rates vary throughout the life of the loan. (True or False)

4. The average interest for a new car loan is typically higher than the average rate for a used car. (True or False)

5. A "medical loan" is a personal loan that is used for medical or dental expenses. (True or False)

6. Mortgage interest is deductible on my federal tax return. (True or False)

7. There is an income requirement to qualify for federal student loans. (True or False)

....

Answers:
1. *False (The average credit card interest rate as of February 2022 is 16.17 percent.)*
2. *True*
3. *False (Federal undergraduate student loan rates are fixed for the life of the loan.)*
4. *False (The average interest rate for a new car is lower than for a used car.)*
5. *True*
6. *True*
7. *False (There is no income requirement to qualify for federal student loans.)*

How well did you do? the more you understand about credit and debt, the better you'll be able to manage your own debt situation. Can you think of any assumptions you might be making that you'd like to explore or research further?

You have now learned quite a bit about debt: how it works, when to use it, which debt is beneficial, and various ways to pay it down. Part of getting to where you want to go is about picturing that destination.

What does having your debt under control look like to you? How would your feelings about debt change in this scenario? What would you be doing?

Key Takeaways

Being able to tame your debt is one of the most important aspects of personal finance. It is very difficult to save money if you have a mountain of debt looming over you. In this chapter, you learned about the different types of debt and that some debt can be a positive thing. You also discovered that there are a variety of ways to get your debt under control.

Here are some of the key takeaways:

√ Credit cards generally have the highest interest rates. If possible, you should pay off your balance in full each month.

√ Mortgages and student loans can help you build wealth in the long term.

√ The "avalanche method" and the "snowball method" are two effective strategies for paying down your debt faster.

√ Other tactics to help you with your debt include debt consolidation, debt settlement, credit counseling, and as a last resort, filing for bankruptcy.

Once you have your debt under control, it becomes easier to focus on other aspects of your finances, such as earning, saving, and investing. The next chapter will explore the ins and outs of the job market and your career.

CHAPTER 5

Employment, Benefits, and Earnings

This chapter will unpack the things you need to know about your job, career, benefits, and earnings. It will examine how your employment affects your personal finances, how to position yourself for a promotion, and what to do in the case of a job loss.

Your work history is a big part of your life in general. According to the Bureau of Labor Statistics, the average American holds 12 different jobs in their lifetime. They also spend 78 percent of their total weeks between ages 18 and 54 being employed. With so much time spent at work, it's important to make the most of that time.

You will learn about navigating the twists and turns and the unknowns in your career. How do you advocate for a raise, and what do you do if you get laid off? There are strategies for these and other scenarios you'll likely encounter.

As you continue your cross-country road trip, think of employment as the fuel you need for your journey. This can refer to the gas or electric charges for your vehicle, as well as your own fuel in the form of food and nourishment. The more and better fuel you have, the farther you can go on your trip.

Ling's New Job Offer

Ling is a marketing manager for a well-established company. She has been with the company for four years and really likes her boss and coworkers. The only problem is that she doesn't feel like she's continuing to learn and grow in this role.

So, Ling decides to test the job market and soon receives an offer from a buzzy new startup in her industry. The position would be a promotion to a director-level role and a 20 percent salary increase. They also offer stock options and additional benefits, including matching her 401(k) contributions.

Ling is excited and ready to make the big move; however, when she informs her current company, they offer to match the salary increase. They also promise to work with Ling to find promotional opportunities within the organization. What started as a relatively easy decision to take the new job has now become more of a dilemma. Ling decides to make a list of the pros and cons of each decision.

For her current job, the pros are familiarity, stability, and security. The main con is the question of career growth. Upper management promised to work with Ling, but there is no guarantee. With the new company, the pros are a better title and benefits, and the excitement of helping a young company grow. The primary con is that this new company may or may not succeed.

After deep consideration, Ling decides to take a chance and go for the startup. She figures if it doesn't go well, her new director-level experience will open opportunities for her at other companies.

Understanding Your Value in the Job Market

The job market refers to any active participants either looking to hire or be hired for a job. Within the overall market, there are a variety of industries, sectors, and types of jobs. Positions range from entry level to managerial to executive level. Levels are typically based on an accumulation of institutional or other education, technical knowledge, years in the field, overall responsibilities, and number of people you manage.

How do you estimate your value in the job market? Your prospective salary, job title, and benefits depend on several factors: the industry, the responsibilities of the job, the city and state you're working in, and the type and size of the employer. For example, an executive role in a large for-profit company will likely pay more than an entry-level job in a smaller nonprofit organization.

When looking at opportunities, it is important to look at the job description and not just the title. Does your experience match up with the duties and responsibilities? Make an honest account of what you bring to the table with respect to your job skills, level of education, work experience, and past performance. How specialized is your expertise?

If you understand the marketplace, then you will know if a job offer undervalues your skills and you can negotiate accordingly. To get a specific idea of how much you could potentially earn in a career, you can check the Bureau of Labor Statistics. They have wage data by occupation, job characteristics, industry, location, and more.

What Are Benefits and Why Do They Matter?

When you're evaluating a potential job, it's important to look beyond just the salary. The benefits that come with a particular job can be just as valuable as the wages earned. In this chapter's case study, the additional benefits offered by the smaller company played a big part in Ling's decision to change jobs. In addition to boosting your finances, benefits can also contribute to your health, wellness, and family needs.

Financial benefits may include equity in the company, such as stock or stock options; paid time off; and matching your retirement contributions. Insurance benefits could include health, disability, dental, vision, and life insurance. Benefits that contribute to health and wellness might be food and meals at work, gym discounts, relaxation spaces, and yoga classes. Additional personal benefits may include tuition reimbursement, family planning services, and child care assistance or reimbursement.

To evaluate a benefits package, it can be helpful to determine what's most important to *you*. If you don't plan to enroll in college classes and you don't have children, then the tuition reimbursement and child care benefits hold no monetary value. If health and wellness are at the top of your list, those types of benefits may be exciting for you.

As you can imagine, these various benefits can provide more than just a monetary advantage. Some may offer you convenience or peace of mind. Ultimately, you are in the driver's seat and can decide what's most important to you.

What Are All These Deductions from My Paycheck?

Your gross income and your net income are two very different things. When you get a job offer, they tell you what your gross, or total, salary will be; however, the amount in your actual paychecks will be lower. The reason is that your employer takes deductions from your pay before you receive it. Some of these deductions are mandatory, and some are voluntary, meaning you have some say in the matter.

Mandatory deductions include income taxes from the federal, state (unless your state is exempt), and local levels of government. They go toward providing needed services for society and the community at large. Part of your pay funds FICA (the Federal Insurance Contribution Act), which goes to Social Security and Medicare. Fortunately, some of this money will come back to you and help support you when you retire.

Voluntary deductions include payments for some of your benefits, such as health and life insurance. If you contribute to your 401(k) or a similar retirement fund, those contributions are taken directly out of your paycheck before you receive it. Although it may not feel great to have more money taken from your paycheck for a potentially distant retirement, contributing to your retirement account early has many benefits. You contribute to a traditional 401(k) before taxes, so it grows tax-free until you withdraw later. With a Roth 401(k), you pay your taxes up front, but you get to withdraw it tax-free later. You'll learn more about all of this in chapter 7.

Advocating for Raises and Promotions

Raises and promotions are beneficial for both employees and employers. When there's opportunity for job and salary growth, employees feel more appreciated and tend to be happier and more productive. Many employers appreciate when employees advocate for what they want, because it tells them what they need to know to keep employees from looking around for other jobs.

Don't be afraid to ask for a raise or promotion. If you never ask, then your employer may not offer it to you. It's important to be able to clearly explain why you deserve a raise. Explain how well you've done on recent projects and assignments and show examples of when you exceeded expectations.

Go into the negotiations with a clear idea of what you want. The average raise is 3 to 5 percent; however, it's not uncommon to receive an increase of 10 percent or more. Do some research on comparable salaries for your job title, industry, and location. Don't undercut yourself, but also try to balance your own best-case scenario with the salary range for similar jobs and the value you've brought to the company.

What if they say "No" to your request? Your employer may simply not have the budget for a raise at this time. In that case, consider asking for other "wins" such as opportunities for learning, increased autonomy, or more flexible hours. Your employer may be able to offer compensation outside of your base pay, such as bonuses for hitting certain goals. However, ultimately, sometimes the best way to get a salary increase is to move to a new company.

COMMON MYTHS AND MISCONCEPTIONS ABOUT THE JOB MARKET

It can be daunting to look for a new job or to ask for a raise at your current job. To help you feel more confident, keep in mind these misconceptions about the job market.

You can't switch careers midlife. Things change over time, including the workplace and your own interests and desires. It's possible to make career changes later in life by getting the training, education, and skills needed for the new career. You may even be able to apply your current skill set to a new field.

One résumé fits all. Each job you apply for will be unique, so it's important to tailor your résumé and approach to meet the needs of that specific role. This strategy could mean highlighting or elaborating on a relevant project or set of responsibilities.

If a job offer is higher than expected, there's no need to negotiate. This outcome may indicate that you miscalculated what your value is in the marketplace. It never hurts to ask, and most employers make an offer expecting you to negotiate.

When the economy is bad, it's not possible to negotiate for a higher salary. If a company is hiring, it knows your work has value and it has decided it can afford you. Employers typically have an additional cushion above their initial offer, so don't be hesitant to ask for more.

Online research is sufficient when researching salaries. Sometimes salary data online is incomplete, outdated, or hard to find for a specific job. It's a good idea to also talk to colleagues or others who work in the industry.

What to Do If You Get Fired or Laid Off

According to studies, 40 percent of Americans have been laid off or terminated from a job at least once in their career. If it happens to you, it's helpful to know what to do in the moment, what your rights are, and what steps to take.

When you first get the news, try to stay calm, take a deep breath, and assess your situation. The difference between being fired and getting laid off comes down to who is at fault: the company or the employee. An employer may also offer to let you resign, or even try to pressure you into resigning rather than terminating you.

If you get laid off, you'll be in a better position to leave in good standing and explain the circumstances to prospective employers. Collect your final paycheck and ask about severance pay. Although severance is not legally required, many employers will offer it as a gesture of goodwill. A typical package is one to two weeks of paid salary for every year worked.

Find out how long your health insurance is covered and investigate options such as COBRA (the Consolidated Omnibus Budget Reconciliation Act) to ensure you have coverage while you're unemployed. If you're leaving in good standing, ask if you can get a reference and assistance finding a new job.

Finally, make sure to file for unemployment benefits. You may qualify even if you were fired, although certain misconduct can disqualify you, such as sexual harassment, safety violations, and drug use. Use the time between jobs wisely by updating your résumé and brushing up on your skills to land an even better job.

Making Sure Your Employment Best Serves Your Financial Health

The tips and strategies in this chapter are designed to help you make the most of your employment and enhance your overall financial health. The earnings from your employment benefit you in many ways, such as helping you pay off your debt, improving your living conditions, and building your retirement savings. The greater your earnings, the lower your debt-to-income ratio, which will enable you to get a better loan or mortgage for your home. And the advantages of your employment run deeper than just your paycheck. In addition to monetary earnings, you may receive benefits to enrich and protect you and your family.

When you examine your employment opportunities, think outside the box, as well. You don't necessarily have to work a traditional 9 to 5 job; there are a number of other types of jobs and avenues to increase earnings. You could work part-time, do freelance or contract work, or take on a side hustle like ride-sharing or renting out a room in your home. Earnings can also come from "passive income," such as returns on investments from real estate and stocks, which you'll learn more about in the coming chapters.

Finally, keep an eye on how your job affects your physical and mental health. if your job becomes too stressful, it can take away from the other benefits you earn. Your job should be there to strengthen your well-being, not wear it down. As much as possible, try to find a job that is right for your lifestyle and your personal goals and values.

Your overall career path is likely to have both ups and downs. No matter where you are in your current employment journey, take a moment to evaluate your situation. What do you like most and least about your current role?

Rating Different Compensation Packages

Whether you're interviewing for a new job or working toward a promotion at your existing workplace, you should be prepared to negotiate the terms if you are offered the position. It would be wonderful to get everything on your wishlist, but it's more likely you'll have to compromise in some areas.

In this exercise, rank how important each item is to you by circling the number that best corresponds to your current priorities. In this way, you can go into a job negotiation understanding which levers to pull.

0 = Not important at all **1** = Okay, but can live without **2** = Would like to have but not mandatory **3** = Very important **4** = Deal breaker if I don't have

Higher salary:

0   1   2   3   4

Insurance (health, disability, life, dental):

0   1   2   3   4

Flexible schedule/Paid time off:

0   1   2   3   4

Ability to work remotely:

0   1   2   3   4

Meals, child care, and tuition reimbursement:

0   1   2   3   4

When discussing a new job, focus on the terms that are important to you and don't waste your energy on areas that aren't as crucial. If you can put a specific number or range on them, that will also be helpful when negotiating.

Your Plan to Get a Promotion and Raise

If you want to get a promotion or a raise, it makes sense to develop a strategy and game plan. Think of this as a sales pitch where you are selling yourself.

Below are some key talking points that can make for a strong presentation. You can use these to develop a script you're comfortable using. Then practice in front of a mirror or with someone you trust to give you constructive feedback.

EXPERIENCE—What have you done over the course of your career to prepare you for this role or raise?

....

....

....

....

SKILLS—What expertise do you bring to the table? Do you have skills that are hard to find or replace?

....

....

....

....

ACCOMPLISHMENTS—What are some recent projects or assignments that you've successfully completed? Were there any "stretch" goals or new responsibilities? How would you measure or quantify these accomplishments' impact on the company?

_____

_____

_____

_____

VISION—What would you bring to the new role? What are your future plans for the company?

_____

_____

_____

_____

Yearly Calendar to Achieve a Promotion or a Better Job

Getting a raise, promotion, or better job takes time, effort, and planning. To improve your chances, you should start planning six to twelve months in advance.

Use the quarterly calendar below to plot out your short- and long-term strategies to reach your goal. You don't have to fill in every box. For example, you may only need to work on your résumé in one quarter or do your research in another quarter. Try to be specific with what the activity is. "Research" could be "Identify the salary range for [job title] in [industry] for [location]."

ACTIVITY	Q1	Q2	Q3	Q4
Skills (What can I learn or build experience in?)				
Résumé, Cover Letters, Reference Letters				
Research: Industries, Jobs, Salaries				
Network: Coworkers, Industry Insiders, Job Hunters				

As you go through this exercise, keep in mind what your end goal is, so you can ensure your activities are focused and continually moving you forward.

What Do You Know about Employment?

Having familiarity with the ins and outs of the job market, employment, and promotions is beneficial to achieving your personal finance goals.

Circle either "True" or "False" for each of these statements:

1. The average American holds more than 12 different jobs in their career. (True or False)

2. FICA deductions from my paycheck are mandatory. (True or False)

3. The average raise is 10 percent. (True or False)

4. I can use the same résumé to apply for any job. (True or False)

5. If I am offered a higher-than-expected salary, there's no need to negotiate for more. (True or False)

6. Forty percent of American workers have been laid off or terminated at some point in their career. (True or False)

7. I can qualify for unemployment benefits even if I was fired for safety violations. (True or False)

8. Whether I'm laid off or terminated, my employer must give me my final paycheck. (True or False)

Answers:

1. *True*
2. *True*
3. *False (It's 3 to 5 percent.)*
4. *False (It's good to tailor your résumé to the specific job and role.)*
5. *False (You may have miscalculated your value.)*
6. *True*
7. *False (Termination for this reason may be a disqualifier.)*
8. *True*

How well did you do? Knowing this information will help you understand job statistics and norms, as well as employee rights as you navigate your career journey.

You started these exercises by thinking about your current employment situation and how it makes you feel. Then you went through some exercises to get you thinking about how to get a promotion, a raise, or a better job.

Now, take this one step further by imagining what your ideal employment situation would be. Think about the job title, tasks, responsibilities, salary, benefits, industry, and location. What would it feel like to have that job? How would it affect you day-to-day?

Key Takeaways

The employment piece of your personal finances is vitally important. It's the main driver of your earnings and is essential for improving the other aspects of your finances such as paying off debt, saving for retirement, and increasing your net worth.

Here are the key takeaways from this chapter:

√ Employment is not just about salary, but also about benefits such as insurance, paid time off, retirement plans, and company equity. It's up to you to decide what's important based on your values, lifestyle, and goals.

√ There are voluntary and involuntary deductions that come out of your paycheck. Involuntary deductions include federal, state, and local taxes. Voluntary deductions include retirement plan contributions and insurance premiums.

√ To earn raises and promotions, you need to prepare by honing your skills, doing your research, and putting together your sales pitch.

√ If you get laid off or terminated from your job, make sure to collect your last paycheck, negotiate severance, and file for unemployment. Remember that you aren't alone and that you do have some control of your outcome.

Whether you're just starting out in your career or you've been working for some time, you can improve your situation. You can take classes, find a mentor, and, when necessary, change jobs.

CHAPTER 6

Buying a Home, Renting a Home

Everyone needs a place to live, and whether you own or rent, your housing plays a major role in your overall finances. In this chapter, you will learn the ins and outs of home buying, from finding the right mortgage to trying to time the real estate market. You will discover how home ownership can help you build wealth, and when renting might be your better option.

As with any long road trip, you'll need a place to rest your head. And the further in advance you plan, the more options you'll have. It's important to base your decision on what you can afford, how much you want to spend, and what your personal preferences are. Some people love camping and being outdoors; others prefer a hotel or staying with a friend. And where you like to stay can change over time.

Likewise, there are several factors to consider when making your housing decisions. Perhaps you want to live in the suburbs, or you want to be close to work or family. Understanding the pros and cons of buying and renting your home will help you make the best decision at each stage of your financial journey.

Brendon and Terry's Home-Buying Journey

Brendon and Terry, who recently got married, just learned that their landlord would be increasing their monthly rent from $1,200 to $1,500. Brendon points out that they will be paying $18,000 per year in rent and asks Terry if it would make more sense to put all that money toward buying a home. Terry agrees, and they start the home-buying process.

They decide to work with a mortgage broker to see what type of mortgage they would qualify for. Their broker, Rhiannon, checks their credit report and reviews their finances. She informs them they would qualify for a $280,000 loan. That would allow them to purchase a home up to $350,000 after a 20 percent down payment. The great news is that their monthly payment would be just under $1,500!

They start imagining life in a new home: dinner parties, cookouts in the backyard, and maybe starting a family. Within two weeks, they find a home for $350,000 that would be perfect. They sit down with Rhiannon again, and after she runs the numbers, the total estimated monthly payment is $2,000. Brendon and Terry are confused, because they thought it would only be $1,500; however, that number didn't reflect property taxes and insurance.

They would be paying $500 more to buy than rent, plus they would have to come up with the $70,000 down payment. Ultimately, they decide that purchasing is the best long-term decision. They can tighten their budget for a little while knowing that, as their salaries increase, the mortgage payments will become more manageable.

How Home Ownership Can Help You Build Wealth

When you buy a home, you're not only getting a place to live, but you are also acquiring an asset, which tends to increase in value over time. According to the Federal Reserve Bank of St. Louis, the median price of homes sold in the United States increased by 60 percent from 2010 to 2020.

Getting a mortgage to buy a home allows you to use "other people's money" to leverage your purchase. For example, if you purchase a home for $300,000 and you make a 20 percent down payment, your equity in the home, which is the home value minus the loan amount, would be $60,000. If the value goes up by 60 percent in 10 years, that will bring the value of the house to $480,000. Your equity will have increased from $60,000 to $180,000, which is equivalent to a 200 percent return on your initial deposit!

Owning your home can also save you money versus renting. For example, there's the financial benefit of being able to deduct some of your mortgage interest and property taxes on your federal tax returns. Your housing payment is also more stable than renting over time. With a fixed-rate mortgage, your payment stays the same for the life of the loan. When you rent, your monthly payment is subject to your lease and your landlord, and it can go up every year. If you eventually pay off your mortgage, you can enjoy your later years with no housing bill or one that's much lower.

When Is the Right Time to Buy a Home?

There are two main criteria you can use to determine your readiness to buy a home: your finances and your lifestyle.

Try to think like a mortgage broker. They review your credit score, credit history, income, debts, and assets to assess your ability and likeliness to pay back a mortgage loan. If those metrics meet their requirements, they will offer you a loan. Then you will need to look at the expenses, both one-time and recurring, associated with purchasing a home to make sure *you* feel comfortable with your ability to afford all the costs.

Typically, the biggest one-time cost is the down payment, which can be as high as 20 percent of the purchase price. Then you have the closing costs, which are expenses such as the appraisal, the inspection, lender fees, and prorated taxes and insurance. Closing costs generally run another 2 to 5 percent of the purchase price. For the monthly expenses, as Brendon and Terry found out, there are more costs than just the mortgage payment. There's also property tax, homeowner insurance, utilities, maintenance, and more.

After all that analysis, if you feel you can afford to buy, then you should evaluate your lifestyle. Ask yourself if you are ready to settle down for more than a few years. Of course, you can always sell your home; however, that has its own set of costs: realtor commissions, fees to stage and prepare your home, and moving expenses.

Can I Time the Housing Market?

If you do decide to buy a home, you may be wondering if you can somehow "time the market," that is, predict the best time to buy or sell an asset to maximize profitability. Typically trying to time markets, whether the stock market or the real estate market, is very difficult. There are many moving parts that can affect housing prices, such as interest rates, availability of homes, and the local job market.

However, there are strategies you can use to evaluate the housing market before taking the plunge. Home prices do correlate, to a certain degree, with the overall economy. If the economy is in a downturn, buyers are less likely to commit to large purchases. You can take advantage of this situation if your job is secure and your finances are in good shape, because you'll have less competition.

It's also important to look at the local market conditions. Review the home prices in the area for the past several years and note any patterns. See if the prices have been moving upward or downward, or if they have remained relatively flat. Follow the local news and research information about the local job market and whether new businesses are moving in.

The risks of trying to time the market are that you either delay purchasing your home, because it never feels like the right time, or you purchase at the peak instead of the upswing. Ultimately, it's often more rewarding to look at your house as your home and not as an investment.

COMMON MYTHS AND MISCONCEPTIONS
ABOUT BUYING A HOME

There are plenty of myths about home buying. Here are some of them:

It's cheaper to rent. Although renting might be cheaper in the short term, buying can save you money in the long term. Rent will likely continue to increase over time, while your mortgage payment will remain the same if you have a fixed-rate loan.

You should find a place first and then apply for a mortgage. It's better to get a pre-approval first so you know what you can afford and will be prepared to move quickly when you want to make an offer.

Being pre-approved guarantees your loan. Once you find your desired home, you still need to go through the full mortgage loan process because your employment and financial situation can change.

You should always go with a 30-year fixed loan. If you don't plan on being in the home for more than 5 to 7 years, then an adjustable-rate mortgage (ARM) may make more sense. ARMs typically have low fixed rates for the first few years, but then they adjust based on market conditions.

Don't buy until you find your dream house. Sometimes it's better to purchase a "starter home" that may not have all the amenities you want, so that you're not overextending yourself on the down payment and mortgage payments.

A fixer-upper is a good bet. Often the amount of time and money required for renovation is a lot higher than initially expected. There is also no guarantee that the work you put into the home, your "sweat equity," will increase the value to the level you desire.

Finding the Right Mortgage

Getting a mortgage is a major decision that will affect your financial life for many years, so it's important to choose the right option. The first is whether to obtain a conventional or government-backed loan. Conventional loans are riskier for lenders since the federal government does not insure them, so you typically need a credit score of 680 or higher.

If you qualify for a government-backed loan, then your down payment may be as low as 3.5 percent. Examples are FHA (Federal Housing Administration) loans for lower-income borrowers or VA (Veterans Affairs Department) loans for veterans and their families.

The size of the loan you need also matters. Mortgage loans above $647,200 are considered "jumbo" or "nonconforming," as of 2022. These types of loans are riskier for the lender, so they typically require better credit and more assets.

Another factor is how long you plan on being in your home, which will help determine whether to get a fixed-rate or an adjustable-rate mortgage (ARM). If you plan on being there long term, then a fixed-rate loan may be your best option, even if they're a little more expensive. ARMs are static for a period, up to 10 years, and then adjust based on market conditions.

To help you put all these factors together, it's a good idea to talk to a lender or mortgage broker. They can review all your options to see what you qualify for based on your credit, finances, down payment, and time horizon.

When It Might Be Better to Keep Renting

Although there are several benefits to owning a home, sometimes it makes sense to keep renting. One of the biggest factors is your time horizon for staying in your home. If you plan on moving again in the next few years, or if you're unsure what your plans will be, then renting will give you more flexibility. You could always sell your home, but it's more difficult and expensive than simply moving from one rental to another.

The next consideration is the strength of your finances. You may not yet be able to qualify for a low-interest-rate mortgage or afford the expenses that go into home ownership, such as property taxes, home insurance, and maintenance costs. If that's the case, you can focus on increasing your savings, improving your credit, and paying down your debts.

You should also weigh the risks of buying a home. For example, although the chances of your home appreciating are good, they're not guaranteed. Natural disasters such as flooding and tornadoes, which usually aren't covered under your regular homeowner's insurance, can be catastrophic.

Finally, consider whether owning a home will make you happy and fit your lifestyle. Owning a home requires upkeep, which may take time away from doing other activities you enjoy. Depending on what your price range is, you may be able to rent in an area you can't afford to buy. This keeps your options open in case you'd like to buy later. Ultimately, if renting makes the most sense for you, then it's the right choice.

Whether you are currently renting your home or you're a homeowner, there are pros and cons to either situation. If you rent, you can call your landlord to fix problems, but they can also increase your rent. If you own, you have an asset that can increase in value, but you must pay taxes and insurance on it.

Think about your current living situation and the various pros and cons. What about it do you like and find serves you well? What about it don't you care for?

Test Your Knowledge about Buying a Home

You learned a lot about the home-buying process in this chapter, including how to find the right mortgage and how to evaluate the rent vs. buy decision. Let's see how much of this knowledge you were able to retain.

Circle the best answer for each question below:

1. **Which of these is a reason why buying a home builds wealth?**
   a. My mortgage loan principal is tax deductible
   b. A fixed-rate loan changes after a certain amount of time
   c. I can leverage OPM ("other people's money")
   d. I can leverage YOM ("your own money")

2. **Which is an indicator that it may be time to buy a home?**
   a. Local home prices are sky high
   b. I just graduated from school
   c. My friends just bought a home
   d. New businesses and jobs are moving into my area

3. **Which of these is a myth about buying a home?**
   a. I should find a place first and then apply for a mortgage
   b. Fixed-rate loans stay the same for the life of the loan
   c. Adjustable-rate loans change after a certain amount of time
   d. The FHA offers loans for lower-income borrowers

4. **Which is a good reason to rent instead of buy your home?**
   a. I plan on staying in the same home for over 20 years
   b. I plan on moving in the next three years
   c. I enjoy home improvement projects
   d. I have been pre-approved for a mortgage

Answers: 1-c, 2-d, 3-a, 4-b. How did you do?

What would your ideal housing situation look like? For many people, the ultimate dream is to purchase a home that they can call their own. However, others may love the freedom of renting and not feeling that they're putting down roots.

What does your dream home look like? Where is it? Are there any special features? Are you okay taking your time to get there? Is this something you want to prioritize as a financial goal in the next few years?

Evaluating Whether to Buy or Rent Your Home

Deciding whether to buy a home or continue renting is a major decision that will impact not only your finances, but your life overall. Although owning a home may help you build wealth in the long term, it can be expensive at the beginning. Renting gives you more flexibility if you don't plan on staying in a location very long.

Taking time to answer these questions can help you determine how ready you are:

TIME HORIZON: How long do you plan on living in this home?

_____

_____

_____

LIFESTYLE: What do you like doing with your free time? Do you enjoy doing projects in and around your home?

_____

_____

_____

FINANCES: Do you have enough money for the down payment? Have you calculated the full monthly payment, and can you afford it?

_____

_____

_____

CREDIT: Is your credit score and credit history solid enough to qualify for a mortgage with a reasonable interest rate?

_____

_____

_____

FUTURE: Is the location one you would be happy living in long term (even if the home doesn't appreciate)?

_____

_____

_____

Your Monthly Budget: Renting vs. Owning

When weighing whether to buy or rent your home, you may find it helpful to calculate the difference in your monthly expenses.

Go through the budget below and input your best estimates for each category. You can get home prices from a site such as Zillow.com and use a mortgage calculator from a site like Investopedia.com. Consider how your other expenses might differ if you were to buy in a different location from where you rent. Perhaps your commute is shorter for one option or you're closer to grocery stores so you can eat in more often.

CATEGORY	RENTING EXPENSES	HOME OWNERSHIP EXPENSES
HOME		
Mortgage or Rent	$	$
Insurance	$	$
Property Taxes	$	$
Utilities	$	$
HOA Fees	$	$
Other Home Expenses	$	$
TRANSPORTATION		
Auto Loan	$	$
Gas	$	$
Insurance	$	$
Parking	$	$
Tolls	$	$
Public Transit (subway, bus, train)	$	$
Other Transportation Expenses	$	$

CATEGORY	RENTING EXPENSES	HOME OWNERSHIP EXPENSES
FOOD		
Groceries	$	$
Dining Out	$	$
Other Food Expenses	$	$
ENTERTAINMENT/RECREATION		
Movies	$	$
Cable TV/Streaming Services	$	$
Hobbies (equipment, memberships, classes)	$	$
Events (concerts, sports, etc.)	$	$
Other Entertainment Expenses	$	$
PERSONAL/FAMILY		
Healthcare	$	$
Child Care	$	$
Education	$	$
Clothing	$	$
Other Personal Expenses	$	$
MISCELLANEOUS		
Loan/Debt Payments	$	$
Donations/Philanthropy	$	$
Other Misc. Expenses	$	$
TOTAL	**$**	**$**

Rating Top Features for Your Next Home

When searching for a new place to live, it's important to know which features and qualities are your personal priorities. These priorities not only will help you make a decision, but also will assist your real estate or rental agent to find the right place for you.

In this exercise, rank how important each home feature is to you by circling the number that best reflects how highly you prioritize it. The below list contains only some of the common criteria to consider, so if there are other features that matter to you, add them in the space provided.

1 = Not important at all   **2** = Somewhat important   **3** = Very important

Price:	1	2	3
Location:	1	2	3
Square Footage:	1	2	3
Outdoor Space:	1	2	3
Age of Structure:	1	2	3
Appliances:	1	2	3
Updated Interior:	1	2	3
Number of Rooms:	1	2	3
Basement:	1	2	3
Swimming Pool:	1	2	3
_____	1	2	3
_____	1	2	3

Key Takeaways

Buying a home is a big decision that impacts your life in many ways. It can be both a personal sanctuary and a great way to build wealth over time. But it's important to understand how the home-buying process works, as well as examine the pros and cons of buying.

Primary takeaways from this chapter:

√ The decision to buy largely comes down to your financial situation and your lifestyle.

√ Home ownership can help build wealth because a home is an asset, with stable monthly payments, that can appreciate over time.

√ A variety of mortgage options are available. They include FHA loans for lower-income borrowers and conventional loans that are not government-backed and require excellent credit.

√ It may be better to keep renting if you don't plan on staying in the same area for more than a few years and you don't like doing your own maintenance and repairs.

Whether or not you intend to buy a home, you need to plan for your retirement. The next chapter focuses on this key piece of your financial journey.

CHAPTER 7

Planning for Retirement

Planning for the end of your work life is like planning for the end of your big road trip. Everything you do throughout both endeavors is setting you up for a successful finish to your journey. Whether you're at the beginning of a new career path or close to retirement age, the best time to start planning is right now.

Not everyone feels financially stable enough to start saving when they are young, nor does everyone receive an early-in-life introduction and exposure to investment best practices. But the truth is that time is your greatest ally when it comes to building wealth, so starting early is ideal.

However, if you consider yourself to be in the mid to late stages of your career and haven't started planning for your retirement, don't panic! It's never too late. Although starting later means some investment options may no longer suit your time frame, you can still begin to save for your retirement. In addition to saving, you can also start thinking about what your budget and lifestyle will look like in retirement.

This chapter will provide you with tools to help you plan for retirement. You'll learn about different types of retirement accounts, income sources, and how to adapt your budget to accommodate your retired self.

Guillermo and Ellie Finally Start Saving for Retirement

For years, Guillermo and Ellie have dreamed of starting a family, and now that moment has arrived. They've just adopted their son, Juan, and become proud parents. It's thrilling and terrifying, especially as they realize they haven't started planning for retirement. They want to make sure that they'll be in good financial shape for their family's future.

They decide to investigate their retirement plan options. Ellie, 32, is a project manager in a growing company, which offers a 401(k) plan. Guillermo, 40, is a public school teacher, and he has the option to open a 403(b) plan. Both can choose between a traditional or Roth option.

This all sounds like alphabet soup to Guillermo and Ellie. Fortunately, their neighbor, Lois, is a retired teacher and is happy to help them navigate the various options. Lois explains that Guillermo's 403(b) operates similarly to Ellie's 401(k); it's just a variation offered to government employees, like public school teachers. The real question they must contend with is whether to choose the traditional or Roth option. Which they choose will change when and how they pay taxes on the income invested in their respective plans.

After reviewing the pros and cons, Guillermo selects a traditional account, because he's older and doesn't expect his salary to increase much before retiring. Ellie opts for a Roth, since she's working toward a promotion and expects to be in a higher tax bracket later in her career. Now that they've made this big decision together, and set up automatic contributions from their paychecks each month, they can focus on what matters most to them: Juan.

What Is Retirement and When Should I Start Saving?

Retirement is the act of leaving the workforce, generally with the expectation that you won't rejoin later. According to a 2018 study from the Center for Retirement Research at Boston College, the average age of retirement in the United States is 65 for men and 62 for women. Some people aim to retire as early as their 40s or 50s, such as adherents to a movement called "Financial Independence, Retiring Early" (FIRE).

Your decision to retire will be based on several factors, including your lifestyle and your financial security. As you learned in chapter 3, compound interest can be a very powerful tool to help you grow your retirement savings. The sooner you put it to work, the more it will help you build your retirement nest egg.

Let's look at an example using a 10 percent rate of return in a stock index fund. Person A invests $100 per month for 40 years and Person B invests $1,000 per month for 10 years. Thanks to compound interest, Person A would end up with $535,637, and Person B would have only $217,187—even though they have the same interest rate. As you can see, time is your greatest ally when it comes to growing your savings!

Below, are two charts generated from the Compound Interest Calculator on Investor.gov, illustrating the difference between the investments of Person A and Person B:

Person A:

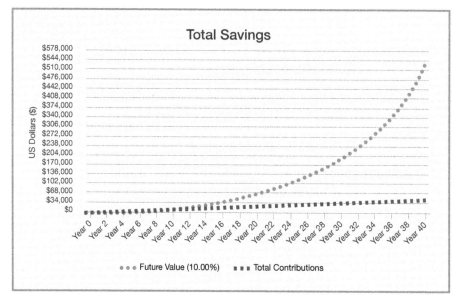

Person B:

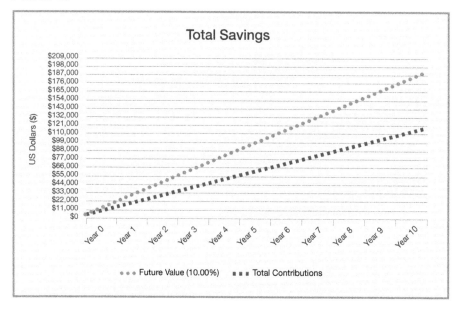

COMMON MYTHS AND MISCONCEPTIONS ABOUT RETIREMENT

Retirement means something different for everyone, so there are bound to be some misconceptions about this part of your financial journey. Here are some common myths about retirement and retirement planning:

There's a magic, ideal number to save for retirement. Some research has shown that you need 25 times your yearly expenses to safely retire. This is a good general target to shoot for, but everyone's situation is different, so it's smart to examine your individual finances.

Social Security will be nonexistent when I retire. The Social Security fund is more secure than most people think. If workers continue to fund it through FICA taxes (see page 74), it will continue to be replenished and will be available for you when you retire.

I'll live off Social Security. On average, Social Security covers about 40 percent of your pre-retirement income, so it's important to supplement it with your own savings.

Medicare will cover all my health-related expenses. Medicare does provide affordable health coverage for doctor visits, medication, and hospitalization after age 65. However, it does not cover deductibles, co-pays, or long-term care.

I'll spend less in retirement. If you plan on being active in retirement, you may end up spending more than you planned on travel, entertainment, and hobbies.

I'll live in the same place when I retire. Since you won't be working anymore, living in a certain location may no longer be a requirement. You may decide to move to enjoy a better climate, to be closer to family, or to downsize to a smaller home.

Standard Income Sources in Retirement

When you retire, the most significant change is that you will no longer be receiving regular income from work. This can be quite a shock at first, especially when you've been relying on that steady income to cover all your expenses. Fortunately, there are a variety of income sources that you can tap into *after* retirement. It's important to know what the various options are, so you can ensure you have enough money to live in a way you find comfortable.

Some people can access their home's equity with reverse mortgages. Others work part-time or have a small in-home business. However, the three most common income sources are investments, Social Security, and pensions. The main difference between these is the origin of the money. Investments come from you, Social Security is paid by the government, and your employer is the source of your pension. Depending on your situation, you could potentially receive income from all three sources.

Investments

There are three main types of investments for retirement income: IRAs (Individual Retirement Accounts), employer-sponsored accounts such as 401(k) plans, and real estate. The first two offer tax advantages while investing in stocks, bonds, and mutual funds. With real estate, you receive income by selling or renting property.

The primary advantages of investments are that you control the amount and type of investment, and there's great potential for growth. The downsides are that you must be willing to set aside part of your income during your pre-retirement years, and any form of investment comes with inherent risk due to market volatility and changes.

Social Security

Social Security is a program that provides income to Americans at least 62 years old who have paid into the program through their FICA payroll deductions for a minimum of 10 years. For every year between ages 62 and 70 that you wait to begin receiving your payment, the total amount you'll receive each month increases.

The pros are that you don't have to do anything special to receive the benefit other than apply for it, and you receive periodic increases to adjust for the cost of living. The cons are that it's equivalent to only about 40 percent of your pre-retirement income, and the fund is starting to decrease.

Pensions

Armed services, government jobs, and some companies offer employees a pension, which is paid income after you stop working. The amount is typically calculated based on how long you worked with the employer, what you earned during that time, and your age when you stopped working.

The pros of a pension are that you get a fixed payment from the day you retire for the rest of your life, and some plans may also cover a surviving spouse when you pass away. The cons are that you have no control over where the money is being invested, and you must stay with the same employer for a certain amount of time to qualify.

Types of Retirement Accounts and How They Work

Retirement accounts provide investment opportunities and tax advantages for saving money during your working years to be used when you retire. There are several criteria to evaluate when looking at each type of retirement account.

WHO ADMINISTERS? You are responsible for your own IRA, and your employer manages your employer-sponsored plan, whether it's a "defined contribution plan" such as a 401(k) or a "defined benefit plan" such as a pension.

WHEN IS THE TAX BENEFIT? You get the tax advantage when you *contribute* to traditional accounts, *or* when you *withdraw* from Roth accounts.

HOW TO ACCESS FUNDS? You can withdraw funds from a traditional account at age 59.5 without incurring a 10 percent penalty, and you can withdraw contributions anytime from a Roth account without penalty.

WHAT ARE THE INVESTMENT CHOICES? With an IRA, you can invest in stocks, bonds, and mutual funds at the bank or brokerage firm of your choice. Defined contribution plans have a limited number of investment options, based on what your employer sets up.

401(k) and Roth 401(k)

The traditional and Roth 401(k) are very popular retirement plans that are available to many employees in the private sector.

The pros are that they are easy to set up—your employer automatically takes the contribution out of your paycheck and deposits it into your account for you—and some employers match contributions. This means your employer contributes a certain amount to your retirement plan based on the amount of your contribution.

The cons are that your investment choices are limited, there may be higher management fees than with an IRA, and some employers have rules about when you can start contributing.

Traditional IRA and Roth IRA

An IRA is like a 401(k), but instead of your employer setting it up and administering it, you establish it yourself with a bank or brokerage firm. The tax benefits and withdrawal structures are the same as a 401(k) in terms of traditional and Roth.

The pros are autonomy and selection. You can select which bank or brokerage firm to use, and you have access to a much wider selection of investments than you might with a workplace plan.

The primary con is that the total amount you are allowed to contribute is lower than with workplace plans. For 2022, you can contribute up to $20,500 for a 401(k) but only $6,000 for an IRA. Also, IRA contributions are limited at higher income levels.

403(b) and 457(b)

Unlike 401(k) plans, 403(b) and 457(b) plans are available only for certain jobs. The 457(b) is offered to state and local government personnel, and the 403(b) is accessible to employees of private nonprofits and government workers, such as public school staff.

The primary benefit of the 457(b) is that you can withdraw money before age 59.5 without penalties, unlike other retirement plans. You may also be able to contribute to both a 457(b) and a 403(b).

One con is that you're unlikely to receive matching contributions, and if you do, they count as part of your maximum annual contribution, which is a cap placed on the amount you are permitted to contribute during one year.

Pension Plans

Pension plans aren't as common in the private sector as they once were; they are being replaced by 401(k) plans that put the responsibility on the employee to manage investments.

The pros of a pension are that your employer has the burden of managing the investment, and once you're fully vested, you have the peace of mind that you will receive regular payments in your later years.

The cons are that you can't access the money in an emergency, and you have no control where the money is invested; it might be directed to funds that are either more or less aggressive than you would prefer.

Which Retirement Path Is Right for Me?

Now that you have some context for the various retirement plans and sources of income out there, the next step is to create the best path for your specific circumstances. Most people will use a combination of the options discussed, depending on what's available to them, including IRAs, 401(k) plans, pensions, and Social Security.

First, choose whether to contribute to any employer-sponsored plans, an IRA, or both. Ideally, you would contribute to both plans, since the more you invest now, the more you'll have later. If you can only afford to invest in one, then you may want to start with the employer-sponsored plan, especially if your employer does any contribution matching. It's easy to get started, and once you do, you can "set it and forget it."

Then you will need to decide whether to opt for a traditional or Roth account. The difference is when you get taxed. The general rule of thumb is to invest in a Roth if you're earlier in your career, and you anticipate being in a higher tax bracket when you retire. The reason is that your Roth investments will be tax-free when you withdraw them, so you can avoid a large tax bill at that time. Conversely, if you are later in your career or you don't think you will be in a higher tax bracket when you retire, then opt for traditional. This way you get the tax benefit now.

Whichever plan you choose, the most important decision is to get started as soon as possible!

Budgeting Your Retirement

To ensure that you can support your desired standard of living, it can be useful to "budget your retirement" by forecasting your future expenses, income sources, and savings. Start with your expenses and consider how they might change when you retire. Perhaps you'll downsize to a smaller home. Since you'll have more free time, you might travel more, visit family more often, and pursue your favorite hobbies. Also consider expenses such as long-term-care medical insurance, which isn't covered by Medicare.

Next, forecast your income sources in retirement. The Social Security Administration website has a "Retirement Estimator" that calculates a benefit amount for you based on your actual earnings record. If you have a pension, ask your employer how much your payment will be when you start collecting. For your retirement, you can begin withdrawing any amount without penalty after age 59.5.

Last, consider your projected savings amount. You can use a retirement or compound interest calculator to help you determine how much your investments will grow over time. The Securities and Exchange Commission has a useful calculator on its site. There, you can enter your monthly contribution, desired time period, and interest rate, and you will be provided an estimate of your savings over time.

Retirement is not one size fits all, so your retirement will be unique to you. The following exercises will help you hone your specific retirement plan. All the hard work you put in now will pay off later when you're enjoying your retirement years!

How do you feel about the idea of retirement, overall? Does it evoke any surprising emotions? How comfortable do you feel about your current level of preparation?

Busting Retirement Planning Myths

There was a lot of information in this chapter about retirement planning, from income sources to different types of retirement accounts. It's important to separate fact from fiction when planning for retirement.

See how well you remember the details by circling either "True" or "False" for each of the following statements:

1. The average retirement age for men in the United States is 70. (True or False)

2. It's better to start investing for retirement when I'm young because of compound interest. (True or False)

3. Medicare will cover all my health expenses in retirement. (True or False)

4. There's a magic number to save for retirement. (True or False)

5. I can start receiving Social Security payments as early as age 62. (True or False)

6. A pension is a "defined benefit plan." (True or False)

7. Roth accounts are taxed when I withdraw. (True or False)

8. 457(b) plans are offered to state and local government employees. (True or False)

Answers:
1. *False (It's age 65.)*
2. *True*
3. *False (It does not cover co-pays, deductibles, or long-term care.)*
4. *False (Everyone's retirement needs are unique.)*
5. *True*
6. *True*
7. *False (Roth accounts are taxed when you contribute.)*
8. *True*

If you didn't get 100 percent this time around, don't worry. Testing yourself and reviewing will help you remember for next time. And the more you know about the ins and outs of retirement planning, the better prepared you'll be.

Checklist for Planning Your Retirement

Retirement planning can seem overwhelming at first, so it can be useful to break it down step by step.

The following checklist will help you work through the various stages, from setting up a retirement savings account to reviewing expenses in retirement. Check the responses that are most applicable to your situation.

Does your employer offer a "defined contribution plan" such as a 401(k) plan?

☐ Yes, and I am enrolled.

☐ Yes, but I haven't enrolled.

☐ No.

If you have access but haven't enrolled yet, here are the steps:

☐ Get the paperwork from your company's HR department to set up your retirement plan.

☐ Determine what percentage of your earnings to contribute each pay period.

☐ Choose where to invest your contributions (see chapter 8 for help with investing).

Do you have an IRA?

☐ Yes

☐ No

If you would like to set up an IRA, here are the steps:

☐ Research banks or brokerage firms to set up an IRA (see page 20).

☐ Set up an account with the bank or brokerage firm from your research.

☐ Determine how much you can comfortably contribute each month.

☐ If possible, set up a recurring investment from your bank account.

Additional costs and items to consider for your retirement life include the following:

☐ Study the cost of living in areas you may want to retire.

☐ Make a list of hobbies and interests you may want to pursue in retirement.

☐ Research the costs of long-term medical care, which isn't covered by Medicare.

Some of these steps are more involved than others, so be patient with yourself as you work your way through the list.

Budgeting Your Retirement Expenses

In this exercise, you will compare your current budget to your projected budget in retirement. This will help you imagine your future expenses so you can start planning for them now.

To get started, return to your monthly budget in chapter 3 (see page 42). Next, consider what your expenses might look like in each category after you retire. Keep in mind that the categories are based on the most common expenses. Feel free to write in or modify them as necessary to accommodate the needs of your personal budget.

CATEGORY	CURRENT EXPENSES	EXPENSES IN RETIREMENT
HOME		
Mortgage or Rent	$	$
HOA Fees	$	$
Insurance	$	$
Property Taxes	$	$
Utilities	$	$
Other Home Expenses	$	$
TRANSPORTATION		
Auto Loan	$	$
Gas	$	$
Insurance	$	$
Parking	$	$
Tolls	$	$
Public Transportation	$	$
Other Transportation Expenses	$	$

CATEGORY	CURRENT EXPENSES	EXPENSES IN RETIREMENT
FOOD		
Groceries	$	$
Dining Out	$	$
Other Food Expenses	$	$
ENTERTAINMENT/RECREATION		
Movies	$	$
Cable TV/Streaming Services	$	$
Hobbies (equipment, memberships, classes)	$	$
Events (concerts, sports, etc.)	$	$
Other Entertainment Expenses	$	$
PERSONAL/FAMILY		
Healthcare	$	$
Child Care	$	$
Education	$	$
Clothing	$	$
Other Personal Expenses	$	$
MISCELLANEOUS		
Loan/Debt Payments	$	$
Donations/Philanthropy	$	$
Other Misc. Expenses	$	$
TOTAL	**$**	**$**

Long-Term Retirement Planning Calendar

Consider everything you've learned about retirement planning and begin to create a long-term game plan. Try to visualize your ideal version of retired life. Using the SMART goal strategy will help you create a realistic road map to retirement.

Start by writing down some high-level goals you want to commit to now, so you know what you are working toward. Then write down some additional milestones that you would like to achieve along the way to help you get to your ultimate retirement goal. Finally, put a rough time frame on when you'd realistically like to achieve that milestone.

Retirement Goals:

I plan to retire at age _____.

I'll feel comfortable with that if I have _____ in my savings account and _____ in my IRA/401(k).

ACTIVITY	MILESTONES	TIME FRAME
EXPENSES	Example: *Eliminate credit card debt*	Example: *In three years*
INCOME		
SAVINGS		

Retirement planning isn't something you do overnight. It is a process that takes many years and requires many choices. So it's important to have a clear vision of what you want. After all, *you're* the one who will be living *your* retirement. Take a moment now to imagine what life may be like when you reach retirement. Where will you live? How will you spend your time and who will you spend it with? Try to put your ideal version of retirement down on the page without holding back.

Key Takeaways

Retirement planning is a long-term process, so it's important to understand what your options are and start making them work for you. The more you know, the better equipped you will be to create a successful plan.

Some of the main takeaways from this chapter:

√ The right time to start planning for retirement is now. The sooner you start, the sooner you can take advantage of the power of compound interest to grow your savings.

√ There are several potential sources of income after retirement, including investments, Social Security, and pensions.

√ Retirement plans vary by three factors: who administers it, when you get your tax benefit, and what your investment choices are.

√ Roth accounts typically benefit you more than traditional accounts if you're early in your career and expect to be in a higher tax bracket when you retire.

√ It can be helpful to forecast or budget your retirement expenses, income, and savings ahead of time.

Planning your retirement is like creating a garden. You plant your seeds now and enjoy the harvest later. The seeds that you plant are like the investments you make. In the next chapter, you'll learn more about what these investments are and how they grow.

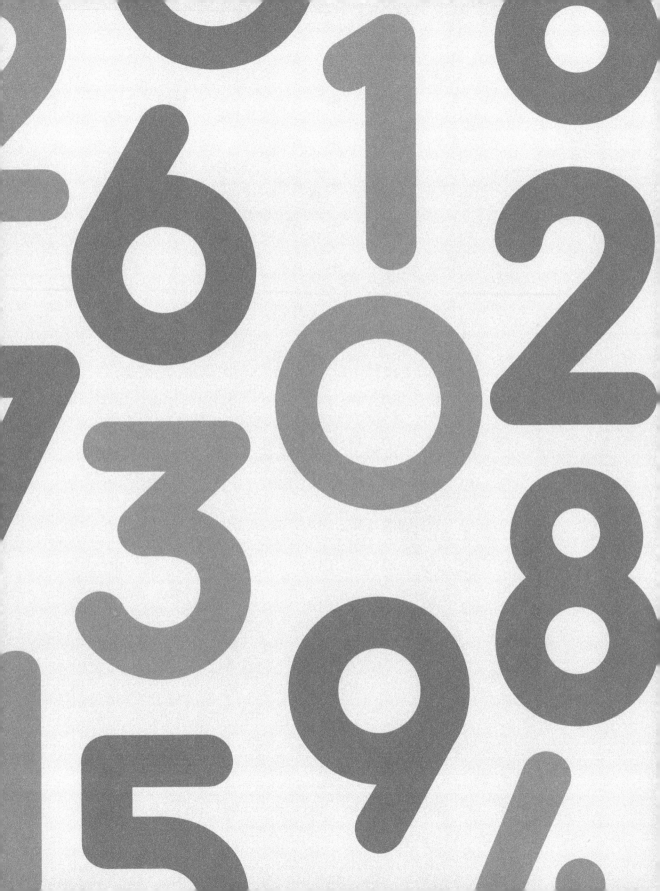

CHAPTER 8

Investing in Your Future

Throughout this book, you've explored the possibilities and challenges of personal finance. You've put in hard work and showed up for yourself and your dreams. You learned how to start a new financial journey by improving your credit and reducing your debt. Then you reviewed options to improve your earnings at work. You discovered how to manage your expenses and make choices that are right for you, especially when it comes to housing. You have also mapped out a destination point for your journey through the process of setting up your retirement goals.

Now, it's time to understand *how* to invest that money you're saving for retirement. Think of this part of your financial road trip as the moment you arrive at the freeway and step on the gas. Imagine the places you'll go, the people you'll meet, and the memories you're creating for the rest of your life.

In this chapter, you'll learn that you need to take on some risk to reap greater rewards down the line. You will discover the principles of investing, popular types of investments, and strategies for investing as a beginner. Understanding the basics of investing can help you make better financial decisions.

An Investment Story of Three Very Different Triplets

I n 1992, a set of triplets—Stephanie, Bianca, and Gisella—were born. Although they looked almost identical to one another, they each had very different personalities!

Bianca was willing to take risks and step out of her comfort zone. She volunteered, traveled often, and loved trying new things. Gisella was conservative when it came to taking chances, preferring to stick to her daily routine and avoid unfamiliar situations. Stephanie envied Bianca's bravery, but she couldn't bring herself to do all the same things. However, she was willing to take more chances than Gisella.

When they graduated from high school in 2010, their grandparents gave each of them a gift of $10,000.

Bianca knew that investing in the stock market over the long term could be very lucrative, even though it carried some risk. She put her $10,000 into an S&P 500 index fund. From 2010 to 2020 her $10,000 investment turned into $41,924.

Gisella wanted to protect her money, so she immediately put it into a Certificate of Deposit, which paid 1 percent interest per year. During the same time period, her $10,000 turned into $11,046.

Stephanie did nothing with her money for the first seven years. However, when she learned how Bianca had invested her money, she decided to follow suit. From 2015 to 2020, her $10,000 turned into $20,559.

Although they had different outcomes, each sibling felt comfortable with her investment decision, because it reflected her personality and risk tolerance.

What Is Investing?

At a high level, "investing" is allocating your money into something that you hope will increase in value. Most people think of investing as purchasing stocks and bonds. Other examples include artwork, real estate, and precious metals.

When you purchase shares of stock in a company, you're buying a small part of that company. If the share price increases, then the value of your investment in that company also increases. The share price could rise due to increased profits or the launch of an innovative new product. Of course, the share price could decrease as well, which would mean the value of your investment would also drop. For example, this can happen due to public perception or if a company doesn't meet expectations for profits, sales, or growth.

When you purchase a bond, you're providing a loan to corporations or governments, who are looking to raise funds. You own part of these debts for a period of time until the maturity date. You're entitled to interest payments, as well as the bond's face value at the time of maturity. Bonds are considered less risky than stocks.

Investing in stocks and bonds can be complex and risky and is typically a long-term investment, especially when done through your retirement accounts. However, you can also invest in stocks and bonds in what's called a taxable or brokerage account, separate from your retirement accounts. These don't have the same tax advantages, but you can withdraw funds anytime, penalty-free.

This chapter will provide you with an introduction, but you should always do your research and consider consulting with a professional if you need more guidance.

Some Basic Ground Rules

Whether you're just starting out or are an experienced investor, don't lose sight of the fundamental rules of investing. These rules have been well established over many decades.

UNDERSTAND THE RISK LEVELS OF DIFFERENT INVESTMENTS. Risk and reward go hand in hand. The greater the risk, the greater the potential for long-term rewards. Low-risk investments include CDs (Certificates of Deposit) and Treasury bills. Riskier investments include stocks and mutual funds, which are bundles of various stocks.

DON'T TRY TO TIME THE MARKET. It's human nature to buy stocks when the market is going up and sell them when the market is going down. Unfortunately, this is the opposite of what you want to do. One strategy to avoid this is "dollar cost averaging," where you invest the same amount on a regular schedule whether the markets are up or down. Over time, this allows you to even out your risk by buying at high and low levels.

KEEP A DIVERSIFIED PORTFOLIO. You may have heard the adage "Don't put all your eggs in one basket." This holds true for investing as well, because if one investment is doing poorly, then hopefully another one is doing well. If you only invest in one company or area and that starts doing poorly, it can drag down your entire portfolio and net worth.

TAKE A LONG-TERM PERSPECTIVE. Because the stock market has many ups and downs, it's important not to make any snap decisions about short-term fluctuations. Going back to 1926, the stock market has had an average return of about 10 percent before inflation, so do not panic if the market decreases temporarily.

COMMON MYTHS AND MISCONCEPTIONS ABOUT INVESTING

For most people, investing in the stock market is not something they're taught in school or at home. If you've never invested in stocks and bonds, then it may seem mysterious at first, but it doesn't have to stay that way. You can start by breaking down common misconceptions:

Investing is for the rich. You actually don't need much money to get started. And if you have access to an employer-sponsored retirement plan, like a 401(k), you already are investing.

Investing will help you get rich quickly. Investing should be looked at with a long-term perspective. The market is like a path on an incline. Sometimes you step down into holes, but the further you go, the higher up you get.

You should pay off all your debts before investing. It would be wise to pay off your high-interest-rate debts, such as credit cards, prior to investing. However, investing makes sense if you can earn more on your investments than your debts are costing you in terms of interest.

You can time the markets. Trying to time the financial markets is very difficult, if not impossible. To do so, you would have to be able to successfully and consistently time it twice: once when you're buying and once when you are selling an investment.

You need to constantly check your investments. Looking at stock market prices every day can get you overly excited or nervous and lead you to make impulsive rather than strategic decisions. It's better to check investments occasionally, such as once or twice per month.

Popular Types of Investments and Their Risk Level

Investments come in many forms and are typically referred to as "securities." A security is a term for financial assets that can be traded and whose values are negotiable. Stocks, bonds, and mutual funds are all securities.

Equity securities, or "equities," provide ownership rights to their holders. When you buy a stock, for example, you are purchasing a share of ownership in a company. On the other hand, debt securities represent borrowed money that must be paid to you. Bonds, for example, are loans taken out by corporations, municipalities, or the government that must be paid back to the holder of the bond. These loans are paid back over a designated time frame with periodic interest payments.

Securities come with different levels of risk. Generally speaking, debt securities are less risky than equity securities. Unlike stocks, bonds hold the promise that the debt issuer will repay their loan. Within each of those asset classes are different levels of risk as well. Some bonds are riskier than others, and some stocks are riskier than others. The higher the risk, the greater potential for bigger gains or bigger losses.

Individual Company Stocks

When you purchase individual company stocks, you are buying shares of a single company rather than buying a fund that holds shares of multiple companies. Although it can be exciting to own stock from your favorite company or brand, it's riskier than owning a fund of companies. The reason is that you're making a big bet that this one company will perform well over time.

Since buying individual company stocks takes more time and research to understand the financials of a company, it's a better strategy for more experienced investors. If you do buy individual company stocks, use money that you can afford to lose if the stock declines.

Mutual Funds and Exchange Traded Funds

Mutual funds and exchange traded funds (ETFs) are very similar. They allow you to purchase a bundle of stocks, bonds, or other securities at one time. Because these bundles provide you with an easy way to diversify your portfolio, they are popular with most investors.

Mutual funds are actively managed by a fund manager, who implements the fund's investment strategy and manages its trading activities. ETFs are designed to passively replicate the performance of a broader index, such as the S&P 500, where your investment gives you ownership in 500 large companies listed on stock exchanges in the United States.

Bonds

When a company, a municipality, or the government takes out a loan, it borrows the money from investors in the form of bonds. The bonds are paid back over time with interest.

Most bonds have ratings that indicate how likely the borrower is to pay back the loan. These ratings come from the three main ratings agencies: Moody's, Standard & Poor's, and Fitch. "Junk bonds" are the riskiest, and AAA-rated bonds are the most secure. As with stocks, you can buy individual bonds or you can buy a bond fund, which is a mutual fund composed of various bonds.

In general, adding bond funds to your portfolio gives you some diversity and reduces the volatility you typically get with stocks.

Cryptocurrencies

Cryptocurrencies or crypto, such as Bitcoin or Ethereum, are virtual currencies that exist across a vast network of computers around the world. They are not issued by a government or central authority like most currencies, which allows for faster and less expensive transfers.

There are some downsides, however. Prices are volatile, based on the number of people buying and selling, and "decentralization" can attract unlawful activity.

Investing in cryptocurrencies is highly speculative and risky, so it's important to do your research. If you do invest in crypto, consider allocating a small amount after you've invested in stock and bond funds first.

How to Invest Sensibly as a Beginner

Investing can be complicated; however, there are several strategies to make it simpler.

AUTOMATED CONTRIBUTIONS: An employer-sponsored plan will invest money automatically from payroll, and you can also set up your own automatic contributions from your bank to a brokerage firm. This strategy makes it easy to invest, because you don't have to think about it or do anything special. You just "set it and forget it."

DOLLAR COST AVERAGING: You can avoid trying to time the markets by using a strategy called "dollar cost averaging." Here you invest the same amount of money at regular intervals, regardless of price. Over time, your investments average out because you are buying at both high and low price points.

DIVERSIFICATION: The strategy of diversification ensures that you're not relying on only one type of asset to perform well. You can diversify your investment portfolio by buying a combination of both stocks and bonds, and an efficient way to do this is with mutual funds or ETFs, such as index funds.

REBALANCING: When you're younger, you can take more risks with your investments, because you have time to rebound from any down years. As you get older, you typically want to reduce your risk. Within your retirement accounts, you can transfer money from one fund to another without being liable for capital gains tax—a tax on the additional money you've earned on an investment when it's sold. The rebalancing process is something you might consider doing once or twice per year.

How and When to Find a Financial Advisor

Although it's admirable and advisable to learn as much as you can about personal finances, there may be times when you feel you need assistance from a professional. Although there's no wrong time to seek guidance, it may be worth considering when your plans for the future change—for example, if you come into a large sum of money from an inheritance and you're not sure what to do with it, or if you experience a major life event, such as marriage, the birth of a child, or divorce. At these times, a financial advisor or planner can help come up with a plan that fits your unique short- and long-term financial goals.

It's important to find an advisor you trust and who understands your goals. As a starting point, you'll want to look for advisors with certifications such as Chartered Financial Analyst (CFA), Certified Financial Planner (CFP), or Certified Investment Management Analyst (CIMA). You can do a free background check on possible advisors with a service called BrokerCheck from the Financial Industry Regulatory Authority (FINRA).

Next, request referrals and ask how long they've been practicing. Also, find out how much time they spend with their clients and whether they take commission-based or flat fees. Discuss what level of advice and service you need, and how involved you want to be.

When making decisions about using a financial advisor, try to assess your options as if this were any other valuable resource at your disposal. Just like any other personal finance choice, what matters is how it works for *you*.

How would you describe your personal investment style? Are you a risk-taker or do you prefer to be cautious? Did any of the investing principles in this chapter make you particularly nervous or excited? What jumped out at you and why?

Test Your Knowledge about Investing

Throughout this chapter, you've read a great deal about stocks, bonds, and investing in general, including different strategies and how to assess the risk level of various investments. Now you can check in on how much you've learned about investing.

Circle the best answer for each of the questions below:

1. **Which of these statements is TRUE?**

   a. Stocks are debt securities

   b. Individual stocks are riskier than mutual funds

   c. Bonds are equity securities

   d. Cryptocurrencies are a low-risk investment

2. **Which of these is NOT a financial acronym?**

   a. CFA

   b. ETF

   c. TMI

   d. IRA

3. **Which of these investments is the riskiest?**

   a. Individual stock

   b. Bond fund

   c. Cryptocurrency

   d. Stock ETF

4. **Which of these statements is NOT true?**

   a. All financial advisors are crooks

   b. Trying to time the market is difficult

   c. I should take a long-term perspective when investing

   d. Diversification is a smart investing strategy

5. **Which of these is a smart investing strategy?**
   a. Sell when the markets go down
   b. Buy when the markets go up
   c. Buy and hold for a long period of time
   d. Put all my money in bonds

6. **Which of these should you avoid doing?**
   a. Setting up automated contributions for my investments
   b. Checking on my investments daily
   c. Asking for referrals from a prospective financial advisor
   d. Regularly assessing my risk level

Answers:
1-b, 2-c, 3-c, 4-a, 5-c, 6-b. How did you do? Keep in mind that just by testing your knowledge you are doing the work to retain what you've learned.

Determining Your Risk Tolerance

Your risk tolerance is a measure of how much risk you're willing to take to reach your desired outcome. When investing, it's important to keep your risk tolerance in mind. It's not the right financial decision if you're not comfortable with it.

To begin gauging your financial risk tolerance, examine other aspects of your life.

Rate the following situations on a risk tolerance scale of zero to five, by circling the number that most closely aligns with your response.

0 = I would never do this.
1 = I might do this.
2 = I can take it or leave it.
3 = I would probably do this.
4 = I would love to do this.

Riding roller coasters:

0   1   2   3   4

Public speaking:

0   1   2   3   4

Visiting new places:

0   1   2   3   4

Skydiving:

0   1   2   3   4

Trying new foods:

0   1   2   3   4

Talking to strangers:

0   1   2   3   4

Gambling in a casino:

0   1   2   3   4

Driving on narrow winding roads:

0   1   2   3   4

Scoring:

Add up your ratings. Keep in mind that this quiz is an informal measure to help you start evaluating your relationship to risk.

0 to 10: Risk averse—you prefer to avoid risky situations.

11 to 22: Comfortable with small, managed risks.

23 to 32: Risk tolerant—you are willing to try things that are considered risky.

How to Evaluate
What to Invest In

When you're trying to figure out what to invest in, there are a lot of choices to review. To narrow it down, it can be helpful to ask yourself a few questions about the industries, sectors, and types of investments that might make the most sense for you to focus on.

Consider the following categories and answer the corresponding questions to help you determine areas for future investing.

VALUES: You might want to invest in areas that are meaningful to you. For example, ESG funds focus on environmental, social, and governance criteria. They invest in areas such as clean energy and companies with a high regard for employee health and safety.

What values are important to you? Are there industries or sectors that do or do not represent your values?

....

....

....

INTERESTS: Perhaps you're interested in real estate, fine art, or collecting items such as stamps or comic books. These are all areas you can invest in with the hope that their value increases over time.

What are your interests and how might they become investment opportunities? Think about things you get motivated or excited about.

....

....

....

PREDICTIONS: What are some trends and changes you anticipate happening in the coming decades? Case in point: artificial intelligence, electric vehicles, or space travel.

....

....

....

There are many different mutual funds and ETFs that represent various industries and sectors. Look for those that represent your values, interests, and future predictions.

Researching Your Investing Options

Before making decisions about investing, do some research. This exercise will help you identify some of the questions to ask yourself and others when considering important financial decisions.

Consider the following areas and answer the corresponding questions to help you narrow down your options for investing, brokerage firms, and financial advisors.

Investment options:

- How much risk are you willing to take? Are you more risk tolerant or risk averse?

  ....

  ....

  ....

- Do you want to be an active investor who regularly looks for buying and selling opportunities? Or a passive investor, where you set it and forget it?

  ....

  ....

  ....

Brokerage firms:

- Is it a full-service or discount brokerage? A full-service brokerage will actively assist you in your investment choices but charge higher fees.

  ....

  ....

  ....

- What are the fees? Fees to be aware of include annual fees, inactivity fees, and extra charges for research or data.

....

....

....

Financial advisors:

- What are their credentials? CFA, CFP, or CIMA?

....

....

....

- What is their fee structure? Is it commission-based or flat fee?

....

....

....

Imagine receiving a letter from your future self, many years into the future, describing your life after successfully investing for the entire period of time.

How will you have invested your money? Where would you be living? How would your successful investments have impacted your life and your family's life?

Key Takeaways

Understanding the complexities of investing takes time, but the strategies in this chapter should give you a solid foundation to work with.

Here are some key takeaways:

√ Stocks are equity securities, which provide you with a share of ownership in a company. Bonds are debt obligations of corporations or governments, so when you purchase a bond, you're providing a loan to those entities. Bonds are generally considered less risky than stocks.

√ Dollar cost averaging is when you invest the same amount of money at regular intervals regardless of price, which allows you to invest without trying to time the market.

√ It's important to reassess your risk tolerance over time. As you get older, you'll want to reduce your reliance on high-risk investments. You can do this by rebalancing your portfolio once or twice per year.

√ Having a diverse portfolio allows you to reduce your reliance on any one investment. Mutual funds and ETFs provide you with an easy way to diversify your portfolio, and they are very popular with most investors.

Investing is a lifelong journey. As your life changes, so will your investing priorities. Plan on being flexible and adjust your strategies when necessary.

Final Thoughts

Congratulations, you've reached the end of the big metaphorical road trip that you've been on throughout this book! Hopefully you feel more comfortable with personal finances now and are excited about your financial journey.

Just as in real life, after you take one epic adventure, you may realize it's time to travel to someplace new. It works the same with your financial journey; you'll likely find inspirations and desires along the way to take you in new and unexpected directions.

When this happens, it's important to be able to adjust accordingly. You can always refer to this book when you want to change jobs, pay off a debt, buy a home, or make an investment. Each chapter will take on new meaning when you're actually going through the events.

It can also be helpful to revisit the quizzes, activities, and prompts at the end of each chapter. As your journey changes over time, so will your answers to many of the questions. Life is a long and winding financial road, and you now have the tools to navigate it. Good luck and safe travels!

Resources

Books

I Will Teach You to Be Rich by Ramit Sethi shows you how to choose the right accounts and investments so your money grows for you, while being able to spend guilt-free on the things you love.

The Simple Path to Wealth by J. L. Collins is a simple approach to investing that the author originally created for his daughter.

Websites

Investopedia provides investment dictionaries, advice, reviews, ratings, and comparisons of financial products. Go to Investopedia.com.

NerdWallet offers objective advice, expert info, and helpful tools to answer your money questions. Go to NerdWallet.com.

Zillow is a real estate website that provides home price estimates, a mortgage payment calculator, and tools to buy, sell, or rent a home. Go to Zillow.com.

Podcasts

Afford Anything is geared toward the relationship between money and freedom. Hosted by Paula Pant at affordanything.com/podcast.

Choose FI focuses on a variety of financial topics geared toward achieving Financial Independence. Hosted by Brad and Jonathan at choosefi.com/listen/choose-fi-podcast.

Apps

Mint is a free app that offers a wide selection of budgeting, tracking and goal-setting tools. Download at mint.intuit.com.

YNAB (You Need a Budget) is for people looking for very detailed budgeting. Download at YouNeedABudget.com.

Brokerage Firms

Charles Schwab provides great educational materials for beginners, so you'll be able to learn all the fundamentals of good investing.

Fidelity is an investor-friendly broker with a high level of customer service, especially by phone, where you can get answers to your detailed questions in seconds.

Vanguard is one of the leading options for hands-off, low-cost index investing, and offers some of the lowest-cost index ETFs.

References

BrokerCheck.finra.org. "BrokerCheck by FINRA." Accessed March 19, 2022.

Brozic, Jennifer. "What is a credit card balance and should you carry one?" Credit Karma. 2021. Accessed March 19, 2022. CreditKarma.com/advice/i /credit-card-balance.

Bureau of Labor Statistics. "Number of Jobs, Labor Market Experience, Marital Status, and Health: Results From A National Longitudinal Survey." 2021. Accessed March 19, 2022. BLS.gov/news.release/nlsoy.nr0.htm.

Bureau of Labor Statistics. "Overview of BLS Wage Data by Area and Occupation (2019)." Accessed March 19, 2022. BLS.gov/bls/blswage.htm.

Consumer Financial Protection Bureau. "Where can I get my credit score?" Last modified September 4, 2020. Accessed May 5, 2022. ConsumerFinance.gov /ask-cfpb/where-can-i-get-my-credit-score-en-316.

Cussen, Mark P. "Top 5 Reasons Why People Go Bankrupt." Investopedia. 2022. Accessed March 19, 2022. Investopedia.com/financial-edge/0310/top-5 -reasons-people-go-bankrupt.aspx.

Experian. "Credit Myths." Accessed March 19, 2022. Experian.com/blogs /ask-experian/credit-education/faqs/credit-myths.

Freddie Mac. "30-Year Fixed-Rate Mortgages Since 1971." 2022. Accessed March 19, 2022. FreddieMac.com/pmms/pmms30.

FRED Economic Data | St. Louis Fed. "Median Sales Price of Houses Sold for the United States." 2021. Accessed March 19, 2022. fred.stlouisfed.org /series/MSPUS.

Giang, Vivian. "6 Incredible Companies That Started in a Garage." American Express. 2014. Accessed March 19, 2022. AmericanExpress.com/en-us /business/trends-and-insights/articles/6-incredible-companies-that -started-in-a-garage.

Hanson, Melanie. "Average Student Loan Interest Rate in 2022." Education Data Initiative. 2021. Accessed March 19, 2022. educationdata.org/average-student -loan-interest-rate.

Investor.gov. "Compound Interest Calculator." Accessed March 19, 2022. Investor .gov/financial-tools-calculators/calculators/compound-interest-calculator.

IRS. "Amount of Roth IRA Contributions That You Can Make for 2022." 2021. Accessed March 19, 2022. IRS.gov/retirement-plans/plan-participant-employee /amount-of-roth-ira-contributions-that-you-can-make-for-2022.

IRS. "Publication 936 (2021), Home Mortgage Interest Deduction." 2021. Accessed March 19, 2022. IRS.gov/publications/p936.

Jarrett, Christian. "How to foster 'shoshin.'" Psyche. 2020. Accessed March 19, 2022. psyche.co/guides/how-to-cultivate-shoshin-or-a-beginners-mind.

National Academy of Social Insurance. *Social Security Benefits, Finances, and Policy Options: A Primer* (National Academy of Social Insurance, 2020). Accessed March 19, 2022. nasi.org/sites/default/files/research/2020%20 Social%20Security%20Primer%20Final.pdf.

Probasco, Jim. "What Is the Roth IRA 5-Year Rule?" Investopedia. 2022. Accessed March 19, 2022. Investopedia.com/ask/answers/05/waitingperiodroth.asp.

Rosenberg, Rebecca. "Can Fired Employees Collect Unemployment?" CO (magazine). U.S. Chamber of Commerce. 2021. Accessed March 19, 2022. USChamber.com/co/run/human-resources/can-fired-employees-collect -unemployment.

Royal, James, and Arielle O'Shea. "What Is the Average Stock Market Return?" NerdWallet. March 2, 2022. Accessed March 19, 2022. NerdWallet.com/article /investing/average-stock-market-return.

Rutledge, Matthew S. *What Explains the Widening Gap in Retirement Ages by Education?* (Center for Retirement Research at Boston College, 2018). Accessed March 19, 2022. crr.bc.edu/wp-content/uploads/2018/05 /IB_18-10.pdf.

Social Security Administration. *The 2021 Annual Report of the Board of Trustees of the Federal Old-Age and Survivors Insurance and Federal Disability Insurance Trust Funds*. (Social Security Administration, 2021) SSA.gov/OACT/TR/2021/tr2021.pdf.

Social Security Administration. "The Retirement Estimator." Accessed March 19, 2022. SSA.gov/benefits/retirement/estimator.html.

Story, Louise. "Anywhere the Eye Can See, It's Likely to See an Ad." *New York Times.* January 15, 2007. Accessed March 19, 2022. NYTimes.com/2007/01/15/business/media/15everywhere.html.

USA.gov. "Credit Reports and Scores." 2021. Accessed March 19, 2022. USA.gov/credit-reports.

Woolsey, Ben. "Average Credit Card Interest Rate." Investopedia. 2022. Accessed March 19, 2022. Investopedia.com/average-credit-card-interest-rate-5076674.

Zabritski, Melinda. *Auto Finance Insights: State of the Automotive Finance Market, Q3 2021* (Experian, 2021). Accessed March 19, 2022. experian.com/content/dam/noindex/na/us/automotive/finance-trends/2021/q3-2021-safm.pdf.

Index

Acknowledgments

This book is a culmination of everything we've learned about personal finances over the past 25 years. We want to thank everyone, but here are some specific shout-outs:

To our parents: Ling, who taught frugality; Harry, who encouraged DIYing everything; Patty, who demonstrated hard work and perseverance; Mario, who embraced life.

To our family, the Plesnarskis, the Toms, and the Millers, for providing us with the family framework to blossom.

To our friends: We couldn't have succeeded without your support and encouragement.

To our teachers: Frank McCourt for inspiring Allison to find her inner author; Tom Molnar for teaching Dylin to broaden his mind.

About the Authors

 **Dylin Redling** and **Allison Tom** are a married couple living in Oakland, California. After working at multiple startups and established companies, Dylin and Allison retired and now write about personal finance when not traveling around the world. Their first book, *Start Your F.I.R.E. (Financial Independence, Retire Early)*, was inspired by their website retireby45.com. Their second book, *Investing for Kids*, has been a #1 best seller in Amazon's Children's Money category since it was released in December 2020.